# GHOSTS II

*The picture of a ghost? Stacey Hansen and her family often experienced strange events in their suite on 108th Avenue in Surrey. This photo, taken in 1994 at a Christmas celebration, shows what Stacey believes is the spectral form of the woman who haunted their home. No family members were aware of anything unusual at the time the photo was taken.* (Courtesy of Stacey Hansen)

# GHOSTS II

## More True Stories From British Columbia

Robert C. Belyk

HORSDAL & SCHUBART

Horsdal & Schubart Publishers Ltd.
Victoria, BC, Canada

Cover painting and line drawing by Suzanne Prendergast, Ganges, Salt Spring Island, BC.

We acknowledge the support of the Canada Council for the Arts for our publishing program.

This book is set in New Baskerville.

Printed and bound in Canada by Kromar Printing Ltd., Winnipeg.

**Canadian Cataloguing in Publication Data**

Belyk, Robert C., 1944-
  Ghosts II

  Includes bibliographical references and index.
  ISBN 0-920663-55-9

  1. Ghosts — British Columbia. 2. Apparitions — British Columbia. I. Title.
BF1472.C3B442 1997     133.1'09711     C97-910620-6

Printed and bound in Canada

# CONTENTS

This book is for Diane

## Preface and Acknowledgements

> Doubting everything or believing everything are two equally convenient solutions, both of which save us from reflection.
>
> *Jules Henri Poincaré (1854-1912)*

One question I am frequently asked by the readers of my first book, *Ghosts: True Stories from British Columbia*, is do I believe in ghosts. The question is not as simple as it appears, for the words "believe in" imply faith in the existence of ghosts that has little to do with fact. I can honestly say that I do not believe in ghosts in this way. To convince me that ghosts are real, I require solid evidence.

When the Society for Psychical Research was founded in Britain in 1882, many prominent researchers believed that the tools of science would soon unravel the riddle of ghosts. This of course hasn't happened, and questions about the nature and existence of non-corporeal beings remain unanswered. Ghostly appearances, it has been discovered, cannot be produced under controlled conditions.

What exists instead is a wealth of stories concerning personal experiences with the paranormal. For scientists, anecdotal reports such as these are the least reliable evidence. Yet it is also true that these accounts cannot be easily dismissed. Can so many individuals who have witnessed paranormal events be wrong? I find this difficult to accept.

One of the problems with ghost stories is that it is often possible to construct an alternate explanation for these happenings. Could not, for example, the ghost of Doris Gravlin, so often seen at the

Victoria Golf Club, be simply evening mist or a trick of the light? This may or may not be true, but it can be dangerous to confuse skepticism with being closed minded. The following personal account illustrates why it is so difficult to reach firm conclusions regarding the existence of ghosts.

On a wet afternoon in February, 1996, I sat in the living room of C.J. Elliot's (not her real name) suburban Vancouver apartment. On the coffee table in front of me, the LED on my miniature tape recorder was lit, indicating that the interview was being recorded. In the background, the stereo played so softly that the music could be scarcely heard above the tat-tat of the rain striking the windowpane.

C.J. was telling me about the circumstances surrounding the death of her son the previous year. Nineteen-year-old Sean's life had ended suddenly, apparently the indirect result of a severe asthma attack. Sean had been living with C.J.'s mother, Debbie, in London, Ontario, where he attended university.

A parent can suffer no greater loss than the death of a child, but C.J.'s pain had been lessened by the fact that she believed Sean wasn't very far away. Sometime before Christmas, a large mobile that C.J. had made began spinning, seemingly without reason. Since it was winter, the windows and doors were shut tight, so there was little likelihood of a draft producing such an effect. At times, the ornate hanging would suddenly come to life and begin to turn rapidly.

Also, during the last three months some of the electronic equipment around the house had begun to act strangely. The family computer refused to boot, the living-room stereo would go on and off by itself, and the video tape player refused to work correctly. C.J. would put in a tape only to discover the picture was scrambled, "as if the tracking was off." However, no adjustment to the controls would solve the problem. On one occasion she tried an entire stack of tapes only to discover that none would work. When C.J. tried to demonstrate the problem to her husband Len, though, the machine worked perfectly and all the tapes played properly. Frustrated, there was little C.J. could do but shake her head.

Another time, Len was in the kitchen washing dishes when a cup suddenly fell from the cupboard near the sink and before continuing on to the floor, it struck a plate on the counter top. Both pieces of crockery were smashed. For the cup to hit its target meant that the trajectory had to be inward toward the wall. One need not be an expert in physics to know that such a happening was impossible.

C.J. was not alone in her grief. In Ontario, Sean had lived with his grandmother for some time, and they had been close. Now Debbie was on her own. During one phone call to C.J., she sounded particularly despondent. After hanging up, C.J. said aloud, "Sean, go to Grammy, I think she needs you." That night Debbie was lying in bed when she heard the sound of a key in the lock. Seconds later she heard the door opening, someone come in, walk across the floor and sit down. The incident was familiar. She had heard Sean do this countless times. When she arose and searched the house for an intruder she found no one. On February 8, 1996, Debbie was awakened in the early hours of the morning by the sound of the television set. Before she had time to investigate, the noise suddenly stopped. Someone had switched it on and then off. Again, she could find no reasonable explanation.

As we concluded the interview, C.J. said, "There's lots of strange things that have happened. Look at that card behind you, it's moving." I turned around to look at the fireplace upon which a number of Christmas cards were fixed. One card directly behind me was indeed moving gently. "It may be a draft from the fireplace," I said, and placed my notebook so it shielded the card from any air escaping from the flue. The card abruptly stopped vibrating.

While I had to admit that it was strange that the draft caused only one card to move — the others had remained still — it seemed to be that the movement had no paranormal origin. I was aware that men and women enduring the agony of a personal loss sometimes read significance into what are usual occurrences. This may have been the case with C.J.

"Thanks very much for the interview," I said picking up my tape recorder from the coffee table. The red LED continued to indicate that it was recording. I put my thumb on the stop button. Nothing happened. I pressed harder. Still nothing happened. I shook the small recorder, and then knocked it against my palm. But the tape wouldn't stop. Finally, by placing the record button between my teeth and pulling up, I was able to stop the taping.

Did Sean's ghost jam the machine? It is impossible to say. Skeptics would conclude it was simply a coincidence. True believers, on the other hand, do not require proof. What I will say, though, is that my tape recorder had never jammed before. What is the real explanation? I can only wonder ...

Coming forward with an account of ghostly happenings takes no small amount of courage, for it is often necessary to endure the skepticism of family, friends and colleagues. Moreover, as has happened in the past, those who have acknowledged a ghostly presence in their house have found themselves the centre of unwanted public attention. I have therefore respected the requests of many who have asked that their names and addresses be withheld.

* * * * *

It is impossible to thank all those who have contributed to the completion of this book. I am indebted to everyone who has offered personal ghost experiences. Others, though, who have not been acknowledged in the chapters of this book include Mike Ballantyne of the British Columbia Folklore Society, for his efforts in aiding my search for ghostlore, and John Adams of the Old Cemeteries Society, for his leads concerning some of Victoria's haunted places. In addition, I wish to express my appreciation to Daniel Marshall, Fran Wagner, Anne Houseman, Wesley Frank, Lynda Chelak, Jack Buquet, Gloria Jean Hughes and Ruth Hoyem for their story suggestions. Also, special thanks to my editor, Marlyn Horsdal, for her work on this manuscript. Finally, I am grateful to Diane, critic, photographer, personal assistant, and life companion, who has contributed so much to the successful completion of this project.

# On the Nature of Ghosts and Their Haunts

As to ghosts or spirits they appear totally vanished from Canada. This is too matter-of-fact country for such supernaturals to visit.

*Catherine Parr Traill (1802-1899)*

This is the second collection of stories about haunted British Columbia. (The first book, *Ghosts: True Stories from British Columbia*, was published by Horsdal & Schubart in 1990.) As readers of the earlier work will note, the stories in *Ghosts II* have a different feel, for most accounts are taken from actual interviews with the people involved. In many cases these ghosts are still active, and thus have a greater sense of immediacy than old accounts retrieved from the archives.

Most of the stories in this collection concern place-haunting ghosts that are heard and/or seen repeatedly at the same location, but there are also a number of stories of presences that haunt people rather than places. Typically, these apparitions return with the purpose of imparting some information to relatives, friends, acquaintances, or occasionally even strangers.

For readers familiar with fictional ghost stories, many of which are set in dusty old mansions, it may not seem unusual that houses are the most popular haunts for real ghosts. People eat, sleep, laugh, cry, quarrel, procreate, and sometimes die within the walls of their homes, so it is logical that men and women continue this connection beyond the grave. Similarly, hotels and inns are popular venues for ghosts, and their activity often involves pubs and restaurants that share the same building. Rather than a casual guest, the ghost is frequently a former owner or one of the employees who lived on the premises.

Another popular site for ghostly activity is live and motion-picture theatres. Ghosts associated with the stage are not particularly unusual; many theatres in Britain and the United States have presences. The most famous haunting of this type is the old Theatre Royal, Drury Lane, London, which is home to at least three different apparitions. British Columbia, too, has its share of phantoms drawn to the limelight, for six theatres in this province are reported to be haunted.

Although it may be that most supernatural entities prefer the comfort of indoor locations, a number of spectres have been reported haunting lanes, roads and highways. The best known of these roadside ghosts is Resurrection Mary who is often seen near the old Resurrection Cemetery on Archer Road in suburban Chicago. British Columbia, as well, has a number of haunted highways and byways. Some stories, like the ghostly hitchhiker supposedly seen near the University of British Columbia campus, are simply unsupported urban myths, but other reports of haunted roads are well documented.

Other locations that are popular settings for fictional ghosts have few real spectral connections. This book, however, contains one account of a haunted mortuary; the ghost seemingly began his activity when the building was still a private residence. Tales about haunted graveyards are rare in this province. There are a few accounts of strange happenings at Victoria's Ross Bay Cemetery, but the stories are fragmentary. A few tales about Kamloops' Pleasant Street Cemetery have been recorded, but the ghost (or ghosts) prefers to haunt nearby buildings. Riverview Hospital, the old mental institution a few miles outside Vancouver, has a number of ghost stories associated with it, but given its sad history, not as many tales as might be expected.

While many readers will be more familiar with the fictional variety of ghost story, true ghost stories are also fascinating. For the men and women who have lived these incidents, there can be no question that ghosts exist. Before beginning this collection of hauntings it may be helpful to look briefly at the characteristics of that most interesting of creatures, the ghost.

## ON THE NATURE OF GHOSTS

Although almost everyone has had relatives or friends describe their first-hand encounters with ghosts, such accounts are not taken seriously by the scientific community. This is not entirely surprising since researchers have long distrusted evidence that cannot be repeated under laboratory conditions, and it is true that most ghosts can't be removed from the locations they haunt. Yet, the lack of such proof does not mean that paranormal phenomena do not occur. For thousands of years, history has recorded accounts of ghostly happenings.

The difficulty with the earliest accounts is that the stories have been blended with existing religious lore. The spirits which appear in early religious writings cannot be seen as separate from the views of the authors of the books themselves. The apparition at En-Dor, which was recorded in the Old Testament, tells more about the early Hebrew religion than about the existence of ghosts. It is only when day-to-day happenings were written down by early historians that the phantom can be shorn of at least some of its religious trappings.

The reason for many hauntings is not well understood. Often the paranormal events may be brief and happen only rarely. Even more strange, in some cases there seems to be no consciousness at all behind the haunting, but only a replay of past events. A number of theories have been proposed to explain this type of manifestation. It has been suggested that certain mineral formations have somehow recorded an event, and that changes in temperature, humidity or atmospheric electrical activity may result in its replay. It should be noted, also, that not all cases involve sightings. One particularly strange event of this type was reported in remote Trail Creek in northern New Mexico. The area was on the wagon route west, and in the 19th century thousands of settlers passed by on their way to California. It is the sound of the settlers passing along the trail that some people believe can still be heard today.

One witness who has experienced the happening on several occasions is a former forester, Mark Newton. Newton's first encounter with the phenomenon occurred in November, 1956, when he had gone into the area to cut Christmas trees. After a hard day's work, he had his evening meal, and then climbed into the back of his pick-up truck and untied his bed roll. Newton hadn't been asleep long when he was awakened by the sound of approaching horses and wagons. "My first thought was that I parked on a road and I must move my vehicle to let them by," Newton recalled later. "Upon looking about, I could see no one, however, on this bright moonlit night." Fully awake now, Newton listened as the noise seemed to be drawing closer by the minute. The sounds were so distinct that the young man had no doubt what was happening:

Wagon wheels were now scraping against rocks, whips cracked like shotguns amid men's shouts of 'Gee' and 'Haw,' while horses laboured for breath. I found myself engulfed in a sea of sounds. Dogs barked, a baby was crying, and people were talking above the din of dishes and utensils clattering and banging inside wagons. At one point a woman's voice seemed to pass right by my ear as she said, 'I must stop and milk Bossy at the bottom of the hill.'

The eerie cacophony continued for about two hours as the invisible wagon train passed over the hill. Then gradually the sound faded in the distance. When he returned to Cuba, New Mexico, the nearest town, he was told that others had experienced the same phenomenon at Trail Creek. Like Newton, local sheep ranchers had heard the sound of the horses and wagons, but nothing was ever seen. While working in the area later, Newton had similar encounters with the ghostly wagon train. He recalled that the sounds were heard only after the sun went down.

* * * * *

Although the various hauntings emphasize the diversity of the ghostly phenomenon, it is true that these events may often have common characteristics. Beyond the sights and sounds that are the primary evidence of a haunting, there is also a range of secondary phenomona. Witnesses, for example, sometimes note a sudden drop in room temperature coinciding with the paranormal event. Interestingly, this is usually confined to a small area of the room, where it is described as a "shaft of cold." There are a number of theories to explain this occurrence. The drop in room temperature may result from the fact that these unseen presences are drawing energy from the room. While ghosts seem to have little difficulty passing through objects, at some level they may obey the laws of thermodynamics.

Electrical problems are also common manifestations of a haunting. People living in a haunted house observe that lights turn on and off for no apparent reason, and incandescent light bulbs and fluorescent tubes burn out before their time. Televisions, stereos, and computers are also seen to behave strangely, turning on and off without human assistance. Some researchers suggest that the difficulty with household appliances may be that the ghost is drawing on electrical energy, but such entities may use this means to bring attention to themselves. It is hard to imagine a better way to announce one's presence than to turn on a television or stereo to full volume in the small hours of the morning.

Another sign of a ghostly presence is the odd behaviour of pets. Dogs and cats may give the first warning that a ghost is present. The fur on the backs of these animals is seen to stand up and pets will begin to growl or whimper. Cats sometime refuse to enter a particular room, even when enticed there by the offer of food. Some pet owners believe that their dogs and cats are able to see what they often cannot: the actual ghost. It may be, though, that animals are better able to sense that a presence is nearby. Like animals, men and women often have some sensitivity to the focus area of a haunting, even when they have seen or heard nothing. The location is described as being "uncomfortable" or "oppressive," and it will be avoided.

Finally, the disappearance of household items can be a singularly frustrating aspect of a haunting. Everyone mislays objects from time to time, but such happenings are usually more common in haunted houses. To make matters worse, in these cases the missing items are frequently never recovered. These incidents may be other ways in which ghosts make their presence known.

\* \* \* \* \*

Although no solid scientific proof can be found that ghosts exist, there is nonetheless a wealth of anecdotal evidence. A poll several years ago in the United States revealed that one person in ten had at one time encountered a ghost. Society's attitude toward this subject has made some witnesses reluctant to go on record with their stories. Because the public often ridicules what it does not understand, these people prefer to remain silent. It is also true that many other individuals have courageously come forward with their personal experiences. This book is about their stories.

# CHAPTER ONE

# Historic Haunts

This province cannot claim to have a long ghostly tradition, but there are some stories that trace their origins back one hundred years or more. There are also many Indian legends of strange happenings that are older than the coming of the Europeans. The following are a few tales that have their roots in the distant past.

## HAUNTED HAT CREEK RANCH

According to psychic researchers, Hat Creek Ranch is one of the most haunted places in British Columbia. In the brief time since the ranch was purchased by the provincial government as a heritage site, many strange incidents have been reported. The focus of paranormal activity is the old roadhouse, which once served men and women on their way to the Cariboo goldfields. Before the turn of the century, the hostelry had a reputation for much drunkenness and violence, and it seems that the tragedies of yesterday cannot be forgotten. At Hat Creek Ranch, the present often gives stark and chilling witness to the past.

\* \* \* \* \*

1

Built in a lush green valley at the confluence of the stream grandly named the Bonaparte River and meandering Hat Creek, the 220-acre ranch is a point of interest for many tourists taking Highway 97 to the Cariboo. Now maintained by the provincial government as a heritage site, the ranch contains many original buildings.

Although the level of paranormal activity at the ranch is high, the identities of the ghosts (there are certainly more than one) who haunt the roadhouse and other buildings remain a mystery. One of the difficulties is that much of what has happened at the ranch has been unrecorded. Given the information available, it would seem that even before large-scale European settlement after 1860, the grassland along this section of Hat Creek may have been used by the Hudson's Bay Company as summer pasture for its horses. Whether or not any buildings were erected on the spot, though, is unknown.

The first independent settler was probably a Hudson's Bay chief trader named Donald McLean. During his time with the Hudson's Bay, McLean earned a reputation for his brutal treatment of the Indians. He was also a man of considerable energy. It did not take McLean long, following his retirement in 1860, to develop his holdings for he knew that the ranch's potential was not limited to producing beef for the thousands of miners attracted to the British Columbia goldfields. Its location, on the Cariboo Road between the gold-rush town of Barkerville and the city of New Westminster on the Fraser River, made it an ideal stopping-off place for the men and women making this difficult overland journey. McLean constructed a log cabin stopover in 1861, but he died before his dreams for the enterprise were realized, shot by Indians near Chilko Lake in 1864, the last European casualty of the so-called Chilcotin War.

Without McLean's drive and vision the ranch soon fell on hard times. By 1867, his wife was forced to dispose of it to another area rancher, George Dunne. Over the years the ranch passed through the hands of a number of British Columbia businessmen. In 1872 a roadhouse was built to serve miners on their way to the Cariboo goldfields. In 1894, the ranch and roadhouse were purchased by Steven Tingley, the owner of the B.C. Express Company, which carried freight and passengers to and from the goldfields. Under Tingley's ownership, the roadhouse was home to a number of

*Hat Creek Ranch, side view. The log building on the right is believed to be the original McLean roadhouse.* (PHOTO BY THE AUTHOR)

lawless characters. "John West, of Hat Creek House, was doing the town [Ashcroft] last week," *The British Columbia Mining Journal* noted in 1895. "No particular damage was done as he was closely watched while here."

The freewheeling atmosphere did not discourage clients, for business at the roadhouse was good. In 1901 Tingley added a new wing, doubling the size of the structure. Yet the days of this kind of establishment were almost over. In a few years, stage coaches were replaced by motor vehicles that covered more miles between stops. The great Cariboo gold-mining boom was now little more than a memory, and traffic along the Cariboo highway was, by 1910, only a trickle.

In 1912 the ranch became the property of Vancouver beer baron Charles Doering who added the south wing to the road-house and turned it into his private residence. After Doering's death Hat Creek House became the property of his stepson, John Basil Jackson, until 1980, when it was acquired as a heritage site by the British Columbia government.

Although there may have been ghost stories associated earlier with the old roadhouse, many of the accounts date from the early

1980s, when the provincial government undertook a major restoration of the structure. During the two years that work was taking place there, it was not uncommon for the construction workers to hear the sound of footsteps from upstairs. The slamming of doors was also frequently heard by the men at a time when no one else was in the house.

On one occasion, a workman was in the attic repairing the wooden siding when he heard a woman's voice calling, "Help me, help me." The sound seemed to come from somewhere on the second floor, but he realized that at this time there should have been only himself and his male co-worker in the building. It struck him that a tourist might have wandered into the building and become lost. Because it was difficult to extricate himself from his confined work space, he was sure his partner would go to the woman's aid. A few minutes later, though, he heard the voice again. Wondering whether his co-worker was playing a prank on him, he moved through the crawl space and down the ladder to the upper floor and looked out the window. From this vantage point he could see not only his partner but everyone else who should have been on site. All of them were too far away to have been responsible for the voice. He searched the roadhouse in an attempt to see if some stranger had entered the building. Next, he went outside and asked the other workman whether he had seen anyone enter the building, but the man reported nothing. The mystery of who made the desperate plea for help remains unsolved.

A story that continues to circulate among Hat Creek Ranch staff concerns the small daughter of one of the construction workers who was living in a trailer on the site. Like many pre-school children, she had an imaginary friend with whom she played. Her mother thought little of these one-sided conversations until one day when the families of those working on the site were having a picnic in the area next to the roadhouse. Suddenly the little girl pointed toward the front porch and said, "See Mommy, there's my friend." On the porch was the apparition of a little girl.

One other tale concerns the families of the workmen who were awoken in the early hours of the morning by the echo of horses' hooves striking the ground. The sound seemed to come along the main road and then turn in by one of the barns. A check of the area revealed nothing. On another occasion, one of the men who was working inside felt a weight suddenly press down on his shoulders. Almost doubled over with the burden, the man left the roadhouse but the weight remained. It was some minutes before it finally lifted.

Nels East, who began work as a part-time caretaker and maintenance worker in 1987, had his own unsettling experiences at the ranch. On days when he was the only person at the roadhouse, it was not unusual for him to hear the sound of footsteps from the upstairs hallways. He would walk up the main staircase, check all the rooms and leave by the narrow stairs at the rear, without finding anyone. At other times he would be standing in the restored bar room on the main floor when he felt a rush of air, as if someone had walked past him. Thoroughly upset, he would turn around and leave.

East wasn't the only person to experience something in that room. In the autumn of 1994, Rod, one of the teamsters, was in the staff lunchroom late one evening when he heard footsteps coming from the bar room. He went to investigate and found the room deserted, but the sound of footsteps on the wooden floor could be still heard. The teamster instinctively froze as the sound approached and then paused. He felt a rush of cold air on his face. A moment later the footsteps continued again, this time walking toward one corner, where they stopped abruptly.

Other ranch workers also found the bar room to be a disturbing place. According to Susan Forccille, the ranch's history coordinator, one of the shot glasses used as a prop was frequently moved to different spots along the bar or placed on a nearby table. No one but the site staff, who all claimed not to have touched it, had access to that part of the room.

Another mystery concerned the door at the bottom of the main stairs that was always kept open by a large wooden block. When East left at night, the block would be in its usual place holding the door open, but when he arrived the next morning the heavy piece of wood was frequently pushed aside, allowing the door to shut. It didn't make sense, for at this time he was the last staff person there at night and the first to arrive in the morning. Susan Forceille has also found the same heavy door closed when it should have been open.

During the reconstruction, workers were removing part of the surface of a wall in the small beer-storage area next to the bar room when they were surprised to discover a key to what appeared to be a strongbox. With the key was a book produced by the Fraternal Order of the Knights of Pythias. The Pythians were founded in Washington, DC, in 1864 with the motto: "Be generous, brave, and true." Membership was open to "any white man of good health," which of course excluded racial minorities and women. In addition, because the "good health" clause was interpreted to mean that only those men with all their limbs could be members, many of the wounded veterans of the Civil War were excluded. Like the Masons, the Pythians had a lot of secret material, and it thus seems likely that the wall was thought to be a safe hiding place for the book and key. It isn't known, however, which of the former owners or managers of the establishment had put the objects there, and what, if anything, they have to do with the haunting of Hat Creek House.

A number of eerie happenings have also taken place on the second floor above the bar room. Early one morning in 1994, one of the ranch workers was upstairs in the computer room near the front stairs when he heard the distinctive tap, tap, tap, of footsteps walking along the hall. From the position of his room near the central stairwell where the three wings joined, he judged the sound to be coming from the 1912 hallway. Alarmed, because no one was supposed to be in the building, he got up and opened the door. As he moved in the direction of the sound he suddenly caught the image of black-and-white clothing. Not waiting to see any more, he jumped the gate that closed off the head of the stairs and ran outside. Some time later the same worker was again in the computer room when he once more heard the sound of footsteps. This time, though, he didn't wait to investigate, but made his way downstairs immediately.

According to Kristina Grant, one of the ranch interpreters, the narrow, dark hallways of the upper floor are at their eeriest not at night, but early in the morning. When she is the first one to open the building in the morning, she notes, "the hair on my arms stands up."

The upper floor of the 1912 wing appears to be a particularly active site. Many tourists report feeling chills when walking down this hall.

According to some, Room 3, at one end of the hallway, is haunted by the ghost of an old woman. There have been two independent sightings of her sitting in a rocking chair, knitting. The descriptions, complete with her hair worn in a bun, matched perfectly.

The servants' staircase leading off the 1901 wing to the main-floor kitchen is also an eerie place. In the early morning when going down these stairs, Susan Forceille has been afraid she was about to fall. "It's like somebody's pushing me from behind."

Not all the incidents happened at the roadhouse. Though the pigs were secured at night in their shed at the back to keep them safe from bears, Nels East often found them the following morning in the pen. There was no way the pen gate could have opened accidentally, and there should have been no other human on the property. On other mornings, it wouldn't be the pigs, but the chickens that were out. Adding to the mystery, no animals were ever missing. At the time, he tried to dismiss these incidents as tourists wanting a look at the animals, but they happened so often that this explanation didn't seem credible.

Something strange also happened in the freight barn, a few hundred feet behind the roadhouse. One of East's duties each morning was to give feed and water to the two big horses used to pull the hayride wagon. On this occasion, though, he was walking past the supposedly empty barn next to the corral when he heard the distinctive sound of someone coughing. He went to the barn to investigate but found no one in the stalls or up in the hayloft. While it would have been easy for him to dismiss the incident as simply his imagination, he noted that the two horses seemed disturbed. Usually when he put out the hay, the big animals didn't have to be called, but on this occasion they remained huddled at the far end of the corral as far away from the barn as possible. East called but they refused to come. He then tried to drive them toward the hay, but they shied away. "Something happened that there was no way they'd go near that barn," he recalled.

Phil Dubroy began as caretaker at the ranch in the late fall of 1993, and during his two winters there he experienced several unusual happenings. On at least two occasions, while he walked through the bar room, he saw with his peripheral vision a bright glow at the top of the stairs, an area that is always dark. When he turned to look at it directly, however, the light wasn't there. On some nights he and his friend, Laurie James, would be awoken by the rhythmic clang, clang, clang of the blacksmith's hammer against the anvil and the swooshing sound of the bellows. When they looked out the window of their trailer toward the blacksmith's shop across the road, the building would be in complete darkness.

One time, during the winter of 1994, they were both in the roadhouse office. As Phil searched for some missing article, Laurie stood several feet back in the middle of the room, waiting for him to finish. Suddenly she felt a sharp tug at her coat and experienced a rush of cold air. Phil wasn't close enough to her to have pulled on her coat, and there was no one else there. The rush of air couldn't be dismissed as a draft; it was an isolated occurrence. Laurie believed that something very cold had come up to her and tugged her jacket.

On another occasion, Dubroy was in the old granary when he had a vision of a body hanging from the rafters. It was only later that he discovered that one of the Chinese workers had hanged himself at that spot many years earlier. Over the years, at least two other violent deaths took place on the ranch. One elderly resident of the area recalled the story that had been handed down about a young boy killed near the roadhouse when he was run over by a wagon. More recently, a German immigrant hanged himself in what had once been the old ranch schoolhouse.

In 1994 a visiting psychic stated that a young servant girl had been assaulted and murdered by two intoxicated miners. Before being discovered by her pursuers she spent many terrifying minutes hiding in the cubbyhole below the stairs where her negative energy still remains. It should be noted, however, that no evidence has thus far been uncovered that such an attack took place. In the meantime the site staff are left to wonder who are the ghosts haunting Hat Creek Ranch.

## MRS. HAYES

Although the Pavilion General Store can trace its heritage back more than a century, the ghost has not haunted the old building long. As far as the owners, Barry and Nadine Schanehorn, are concerned, the presence is not an unwelcome guest.

\* \* \* \* \*

The Pavilion General Store on Highway 99, about 25 miles west of Hat Creek Junction, has had a long, colourful history. Built in 1862 as a stopover for travellers taking the Harrison-Lillooet route to the goldfields, the store still dispenses fresh coffee, cigarettes, and other items to modern tourists exploring one of the province's lesser-travelled highways. Today it claims to be the oldest general store in the province.

Over the years many renovations have been made to the building. In the 1930s, an addition was completed on the west side of the structure that is now used as the kitchen and living room of the present owners. The area above the store, which was part of the original roadhouse, is used as bedrooms for Barry and Nadine Schanehorn and their guests. The Schanehorns, who were from Alberta, bought the store in 1992 as a result of a chance stop there while travelling in the region. The couple was taken by the fascinating old place, and the owners were willing to sell.

Although the store is more than 130 years old, the ghost, at least according to local legend, is fairly new. She is said to be Mrs. Hayes, a woman who owned the store about half a century ago. She was deeply attached to the property and apparently has been reluctant to leave.

Before moving in, the Schanehorns had heard a number of stories from the previous owners, Tony and Trudy Takacs. In their time, a number of strange occurrences had taken place. One day Trudy was sitting in the store having coffee with one of the women who lived nearby when suddenly all the packages of cigarettes that had been on the shelf behind the counter tumbled to the floor. Trudy could think of no explanation — the packages had been held in place by a wooden lip on the shelf. It would have been necessary for them to fall up and over the barrier.

On another occasion, Tony had gone to bed before his wife and had fallen asleep immediately. He awoke in the middle of the night with his arm over what he thought was Trudy under the covers next to him. As he went down the hall to the bathroom, he was aware of the sound of the television coming from the living room. Thinking his wife had forgotten to turn off the TV when she had come to bed, he went downstairs. To his surprise he found Trudy asleep on the couch. Perplexed, he asked her if she had come down to the living room when he had gone to the toilet. "No," she said. "I fell asleep down here while I was watching TV." Tony Takacs had apparently awoken with his arm over the ghost.

Soon after moving in, Barry had a feeling he and Nadine were not alone in the store. Tela, their dog, also seemed to sense something strange. Often during the day or evening, the German shepherd would get up and walk toward the stairs leading to the second floor. As the couple watched, the fur on the animal's neck would stand on end.

Later, Barry's mother, who lived in Alberta, came to visit, and one afternoon, when Barry and Nadine were working behind the counter, Connie Konkin, a school teacher from Lillooet, stopped by on her way home. The Schanehorns were chatting with their customer when suddenly they heard the sound of footsteps along the hallway upstairs.

"Who's that?" Connie asked.

"That's probably Mom," Nadine answered.

"That's not her," Barry said. "She's sleeping on the chesterfield."

Barry went to the room next door and sure enough, his mother was lying on the living-room couch, fast asleep.

*The Pavilion General Store.* (COURTESY OF DIANE BELYK)

A search of the upstairs bedrooms and hall revealed no one. The age of the building meant that footsteps were easily recognized, for the floorboards protested under the weight of a human body. Other minor happenings in the old store are quite common. Windows left open to provide ventilation on hot summer nights are found closed in the morning. Similarly, curtains that have been shut in the evening are found open the next day. One of the corner bedrooms has also been noted to be exceptionally cold, in both winter and summer. While no one died violently, a former resident endured a long and difficult death in that bedroom.

Several of the local native people have asked Barry if he wishes them to perform a smudging ceremony to remove the spirit, but as far as Barry is concerned, the ghost is welcome to stay. As long as she causes no trouble, he says, Mrs. Hayes has every right to remain. After all, she was there first.

## THE MOUSE WOMAN OF KITSELAS CANYON

In the legends of the Indian nations of the Northwest Coast, Mouse Woman is a powerful spirit who guides travellers between one world and another. According to the Tsimshian people, she inhabits Kitselas Canyon on the Skeena River, a few miles northeast of Terrace. For two young archeology students working in the area, Mouse Woman suddenly became more than simply the stuff of myth.

\* \* \* \* \*

During the summer of 1982, a number of archeology students were working on a university-sponsored excavation in Kitselas Canyon. For some reason the young people found the Mouse Woman legends amusing — Tsimshian stories claimed that she was able at will to transform herself from a mouse into a tiny old lady — and there were many jokes at her expense.

One evening after work, two students, Ian McEwan and Amanda Murray (not their real names), decided to spend the night away from the dig, at a place in the canyon renowned for its natural beauty. Using Ian's van, the pair picked up supplies in Terrace and by the time they had hiked down the trail to the spot where they planned to camp, it was growing dark. They had quickly set up their tent, built a campfire, and begun to prepare dinner when both were suddenly aware of a strange feeling. It was a strong, palpable fear that seemed to come out of nowhere. Ian knew that they were in the presence of something very powerful. Although nothing was said to their unseen visitor, neither Ian nor Amanda had the slightest doubt that this was the Mouse Woman spirit. Her presence seemed to be almost physical, as if a great burden had been placed on their shoulders.

With the weight still pressing down on them, the pair got up, broke camp, climbed back in the van and drove to Terrace where they found a brightly lit Chinese restaurant. "The presence stayed with us until we had been there about ten minutes," Ian said. "Then all of a sudden it was gone, just like a cloud going away from overhead, [and] the sun coming out." The incident was very disturbing for both young people, but neither Ian nor Amanda brought it up during their remaining time at the dig.

After that summer the two students went on with their lives and lost contact with each other. About eight years later, however, Ian happened to meet Amanda on Pender Island, where he was surprised to note the change in his friend. A one-time committed Roman Catholic, Amanda had forsaken her former religion and was now a student of New Age beliefs. She told Ian she was taking a course in women's spirituality in Victoria and during the sessions had astral-travelled to Kitselas Canyon. There at the archeological site dug nine feet into the canyon, she communed with Mouse Woman. When Ian reminded her of their experience together in the canyon, Amanda said that was why she was drawn back to that remote spot.

While the incident was something Ian never forgot, the tangible presence of Mouse Woman had an even greater effect on his friend. Amanda's faith in the world she had known since childhood was severely shaken. She had been changed fundamentally by her encounter with that ancient spirit of Kitselas Canyon.

## GUISACHAN'S PHANTOM HORSE AND CARRIAGE

Evergreens imported from England, which Lady Aberdeen chose to plant along the long lane leading to her house, gave the

*Guisachan House, built for Lord and Lady Aberdeen, is now a restaurant.*
(Courtesy of Diane Belyk)

estate its name. When John Gordon, Lord Aberdeen, and Lady Aberdeen bought the property near Lake Okanagan, in the early 1890s, they called it "Guisachan," which in Gaelic means "place of firs." The original trees have long since died and been replaced by a hardy species of Canadian cedar, but it seems that an echo of the past is connected to this tree-lined lane. According to legend, sometimes on clear nights when the moon is full, a horse and carriage can be heard coming down the Avenue of Cedars.

The Aberdeens did not own the property long before it was sold to Okanagan Valley residents. William Cameron recalls living in the house as a child, but does not remember hearing the sound of the horse and carriage coming up the driveway. His parents, though, apparently heard it.

The old estate, which is now the Guisachan Heritage Park, is not far from downtown Kelowna. Site manager C. D. Macdougall states that he has heard the sound of horses' hooves and carriage wheels half way down the lane, not once but many times. Rather than frightening, though, he finds the sound intriguing. Why this

*Guisachan's Avenue of Cedars, where a horse and carriage are heard but never seen.* (COURTESY OF DIANE BELYK)

horse and carriage repeats its nocturnal journey isn't known, but some local residents believe that it was on its way to a party at the house. No one knows whether the gathering was during the Aberdeens' time or not, but the event has left a lasting imprint on the fabric of time.

## THE LEGEND OF CHUTE LAKE'S PHANTOM PIPER

As is often the case with folk tales, many of the details of Kevin McDermid's life and death have been lost. The story, though, with its elements of romance and tragedy, continues to capture the imagination of contemporary British Columbians.

\* \* \* \* \*

Kevin McDermid was a young man who came to British Columbia from Scotland during the gold rush and found employment constructing the Dewdney Trail that linked the towns of

14

Hope and Princeton. Unfortunately for McDermid, a powder blast in 1860 took off his left leg. Although his employment prospects were now limited, he was a resourceful person, and he soon built a homestead in the Chute Lake area, near the south end of Lake Okanagan. When his house was completed he sent to Scotland for his wife and the couple eked out a living in this isolated spot.

McDermid's great joy was to play the bagpipes he had brought with him. When he could spare the time, he would go up into the hills and play the old Scottish tunes he and his wife loved so much. As the music travelled down the valley it seemed to take on a richness of tone that touched the heart of anyone passing by.

Not many people heard McDermid's playing, for few endured the difficult ride on horseback to Chute Lake. The price of their isolation was made clear when McDermid's wife suddenly became ill. She was too sick to move, and her only hope was for McDermid to pay the cost of bringing in a physician from Princeton. McDermid collected what money he could, but it was not enough. He had to watch her die, slowly and in pain, far from medical help.

After her death, McDermid was rarely seen. When time had passed without word from him, his neighbours became increasingly concerned, and a few men made their way along the rough trail leading to his homestead. They found that his cabin was deserted. Outside the door was the body of his horse, still tethered to the hitching post. On a hill some distance from the cabin, his neighbours found his much-loved bagpipes, but there was no sign of Kevin McDermid.

It is said, in the Chute Lake area, that on a clear night you may hear the chanting of McDermid's pipes. And if you happen to be at the right spot when the moon is full, you may even catch a glimpse of the man himself, atop a hill, playing a melancholy air to his long-lost love.

\* \* \* \* \*

Many of British Columbia's oldest residences have also gained a reputation for being haunted. Victoria's Tod House, Point Ellice House, and Hatley Park as well as New Westminster's Irving House are four haunted homes that are now open to the public. (These tales are included in *Ghosts: True Stories from British Columbia*.)

15

# CHAPTER TWO

# Haunted Houses

A home is often imagined to be the foundation of North American life, a place of security and protection for all. Yet it is true that a home may also have spirit inhabitants that can be very frightening indeed. Here are some stories of British Columbia's house-haunting ghosts.

## MARY'S RING

The people continue to live in the house mentioned in this story, and have requested that their names and the names of others, as well as the exact location of the house, not be published. Given the paranormal activity that has occurred there during the past several years, they are afraid that their home will attract the unwanted attention of the press and public.

\* \* \* \* \*

The house in the Fraser Valley community of Langley had been on the market only a short time, in the summer of 1992, when Victor and Pamela Oulton (not their real names) were shown the listing. The contemporary-looking, three-bedroom dwelling in a quiet subdivision close to schools and stores seemed to have everything they wanted. It was only a few years old and, from the outside at least, had a bright, airy appearance. The thought that the house was in any way peculiar was far from their minds when they signed the purchase papers.

The Oultons were not disposed to believe in the paranormal. For Victor, particularly, the notion that ghosts existed was absurd. He had a scientific turn of mind that demanded logic, and as far as he was concerned, there was certainly no proof that ghosts were real. For this reason, he had no difficulty explaining the loud metallic clang that was heard sometimes from the basement: it was nothing more than the expansion and contraction of the furnace pipes as they heated and cooled. Although Pamela found the noise disturbing, Victor's explanation seemed reasonable. As the months passed, though, even Victor became less sure of the source of the sounds. The clanging sound was only one part of a litany of bizarre happenings that had taken place within the couple's home.

Victor feels that the removal of the tree at the front of his house marked the beginning of the strange happenings at his new home. The Oultons had been living in their house less than a month when he decided to remove a large red maple tree from the front yard. The tree had been planted five years earlier during the original landscaping, and there was now reason to fear that its root system would begin to clog the water pipes or damage the house foundation. Victor chopped the tree down and dug up the roots. The task was more difficult than he had thought. What remained of the tree below ground clung tenaciously to the soil, and in the end he had to haul out the main root by means of a chain secured to his truck. He filled in the hole and after the job was completed, he put the task out of his mind.

Not long after the maple tree had been removed, the Oultons began to notice that their big black Labrador retriever, Trina, was acting strangely. Sometimes at night the dog would suddenly stir from her mat in the hallway and stare intently into the kitchen. Trina's eyes seemed to be following something moving around the room, but whatever it was, it couldn't be seen by Victor or Pamela. At other times Trina would move restlessly around her spot in the hallway and utter spine-chilling howls.

When Victor and Pamela moved in, they allowed Dawn, one of their co-workers — Victor and Pamela work for the same employer — to rent the finished basement for a nominal charge. Although the accommodation was partly self-contained, Dawn used the shower and kitchen facilities upstairs. The arrangement seemed to work satisfactorily for the first few days, but while Victor and Pamela attempted to conserve electricity by being "power smart," Dawn apparently wasn't so inclined. The Oultons were continually reminding their tenant to turn the lights out after she had left a room. Dawn, for her part, denied being guilty of these infractions, and although the incidents were minor, tension developed between the three people. Dawn had been there less than a month when she moved out.

After their experience with Dawn, the Oultons decided never to have a tenant again, but when Jan, another co-worker, approached them asking for a place to stay, they changed their minds. Jan had been living there about a month when she brought home a kitten to keep her company. The little creature had hardly set foot in her apartment when it began to act strangely. It shredded Jan's sofa and chairs and scratched the furniture. If anyone approached it, the kitten would strike out with such ferocity that it drew blood. On other occasions it would run around the room uncontrollably, jumping from the floor to the furniture. Before long it was clear to Jan that she couldn't continue to put up with the kitten's behaviour, and it was returned to the SPCA.

During this time Victor and Pamela were experiencing problems with their electronic equipment. The video-cassette recorder and compact-disc player worked only intermittently, while the clothes dryer stopped entirely. Lights were another irritation, for bulbs were often burning out.

The freezer, a wedding gift from Pamela's parents, was the centre of another mystery. One day Victor discovered that the temperature control had been turned to the "full on" position. A similar incident happened to the hot-water tank. When the water from the faucet was suddenly much hotter, Victor found that the temperature regulator on the tank had been turned to the highest setting that was possible. Since it was in the basement, Victor questioned Jan about whether she had turned up the temperature, but she emphatically denied touching the regulator.

The Oultons were also aware of an unpleasant odour that sometimes invaded individual rooms. It was a very heavy, earthy smell that was reminiscent of decay. It seemed unusual that the odour didn't permeate all areas of a room, but remained in a narrow column. Strange also was the fact that it appeared in different areas of the house and never seemed to last long. The Oultons never were able to discover the source of the odour.

While the Oultons were very fond of their dog, Trina's habit of digging holes in the back yard was bothersome. To prevent this, Victor decided, in early 1993, to put bricks down in the back yard. He was levelling an area where Trina had dug a hole when he noticed something shining in the light. It was a ring. Thinking that it was some child's toy, he put it aside and continued working. Only later, when he took the object inside and washed it off, did he realize the importance of his find. The ring was obviously no child's novelty. The style was old-fashioned, with one large diamond between two smaller stones in a white-gold setting. It was still possible to read the 14-karat mark on the inside of the band. Victor gave the ring to his wife who had it re-sized, but although

*Mary's Ring.* (Photo by the Author)

19

the ring was pleasing to the eye, Pamela never felt comfortable wearing it, and in the end it remained in a drawer.

About this time, the Oultons were experiencing a run of misfortune. Victor came down with a kidney infection that left him seriously ill, and it was months before he recovered. The couple desperately wanted a family, and Pamela suffered the first of what would be three miscarriages. On another occasion, shortly after leaving home, Victor's truck was struck by another vehicle. While it was badly damaged, he escaped with only minor injuries. An ongoing problem they faced was money. Although the Oultons had good jobs, it was impossible to save anything — automobile repairs and other unanticipated costs took all their income.

Another difficulty that left the Oultons perplexed was the mysterious disappearances of household items. Although Victor and Pamela didn't regard themselves as careless, objects around the house would suddenly vanish. House keys, car keys and Victor's watches were frequently on the Oultons' missing list. Only one of three watches turned up again, and that in the unlikeliest of spots. Victor found it laid out neatly on a shelf in one of the kitchen cupboards.

One of the objects to disappear was his talking key chain, an electronic novelty Victor kept in his pocket. The little device had four coloured buttons ranging from white to red, each colour producing a different profanity, from "mild" to "hot." Instead of cursing other drivers himself, Victor simply pressed one of the buttons. While the item was nothing more than a joke, he was in the habit of carrying it with him. There came a time, however, when Victor could no longer find the key chain. He thought little of it until one evening in February, 1995, when he was alone in the living room and happened to notice that Trina had crumpled her mat in the hall. As he bent down to straighten it, he suddenly heard the familiar tiny metallic voice speak the "hot" four-letter word coming from the next room. He went to the kitchen and began opening cupboards in an effort to find where the sound came from, and after several minutes he found the plastic novelty behind a mail rack. It was not visible and only by putting his hand inside the rack and feeling around was he able to find it. He wondered why it began speaking at that moment, for apparently it had remained silent in the mail rack for months.

As time passed, other unsettling incidents took place. One night Victor and Pamela had gone to bed but were not yet asleep when they were disturbed by a loud clatter, as if someone had with great force thrown a set of keys against their bedroom wall. The Oultons sat up in bed and put the light on, but there was nothing to be seen. When Victor got up, he found his own keys where he had placed them.

Jan, too, was aware of a disturbing presence in the house. When she came home to her basement apartment she would frequently hear noises upstairs. Thinking someone was home she would go up to see Victor or Pamela, but no one would be there. One night when she returned home late from a date she retired to bed, but before falling to sleep, she happened to glance at the door in the half-light of her room. There she noticed what appeared to be a small, round, black hole in the middle of the wood facing her. Jan was angry, because she had no idea how such a thing had happened, and she felt responsible. But as she watched, the hole began to get larger. She quickly closed her eyes and shook her head, and when she opened her eyes again, it was gone.

Although it was difficult to point to the reason, relations between the Oultons and their tenant were becoming increasingly strained. As with Dawn earlier, petty disagreements seemed to get blown out of proportion. By the spring of 1994, Jan had angrily moved out.

Meanwhile, the Oultons continued to undergo what Victor came to call "strange days." Located as it was in the back of the house, the Oultons' kitchen seemed to be the scene of much paranormal activity. One evening Victor was tidying up when he remembered he had something to tell Pamela who was riding the exercise bike downstairs. Before going down, he stood the broom he had been using against the kitchen table. He had been downstairs only a couple of minutes when he and Pamela heard a loud whack coming from above.

When Victor ran up the stairs into the hall, he could see the broom he had left in the kitchen now lying in the living room. It was flat on the floor, at least 20 feet away from where he had left it. Victor's first thought was that the broom had fallen over, but when he re-enacted the event, the wooden handle made no more than a sharp thud as it hit the floor. Only when he took the broom and struck it with full force against the floor could he repeat the loud whack. But he knew, even had the broom simply fallen over, it wouldn't explain how it moved from the kitchen to the living room.

The house had a finished basement with little space for storage, which was a problem for the couple. One of the few unused locations was the area under the stairs, which the builder had simply closed in with dry-wall. Victor decided to turn this area into a storage closet. As he removed the panel, he was struck by a gust of warm wind. He considered the matter for a moment; it seemed impossible that a blast of air would be felt in that space, for the area was sealed tightly. It should have held only dead air. However, given the other mysteries associated with the house, Victor wasn't inclined to think much about it. After the area was converted into a closet, no more air gusts were felt, and the incident was all but forgotten.

Some months later Victor was alone in the house, sitting in the living room watching a hockey game. Something caught his eye: it was a small black object streaking across the kitchen floor and ricocheting off the wall. When he went to investigate he found the lid of the coffee maker lying on the floor. Victor was puzzled. He took the lid and tried to duplicate the skimming action he had seen, but he couldn't repeat it. For Victor it was clear that whatever produced this incident was aware of what was on television — the lid had behaved like a hockey puck.

On another evening, Victor was in the living room when he happened to glance up at a small framed picture leaning against a plant on the mantel. It was a photo of the couple on their wedding day. As Victor watched, the picture suddenly flipped forward and fell to the carpet. That it had pitched over made no sense, Victor realized, for it should have simply slid down on its back. The top of the photograph had fallen forward *against* the force of gravity.

On Christmas Eve, two years after moving in, Victor and Pamela had retired to bed after a busy day when they were suddenly aware of the sound of their pots and pans rattling. The noise lasted only about 30 or 40 seconds, but was quite loud. When Victor reached the kitchen the sound had stopped. The cause might have been a small earthquake, but there were no reports on the news of local seismic activity.

A disturbing incident occurred one afternoon when Victor returned to an empty house — Pamela was at work. After coming in the front door he glanced up to see a man looking down at him from the top of the stairs. His visitor was very tall and slender, wearing a white shirt, an old-fashioned black broadcloth coat and wide-brimmed hat. Before quickly disappearing, the man smiled down at him through a mouthful of broken teeth. He did not feel threatened by the old man's visit — Victor took him to be well past middle age — but the incident was nonetheless unsettling. Not long afterward, Pamela was in the bathroom with the door open when she saw a black shape glide by. When she looked into the hall nothing was there.

In February, 1995, Victor and Pamela were shaken by another strange happening. At the funeral of an elderly family friend, Victor was approached by his cousin, Libby. Victor and Libby had never been close, so he was surprised when she said, "I have to see you." When Libby arrived at the Oultons' home, she was visibly distraught. During her tour of the house she picked up a large, sand-cast statue of a dog, and said, "Oh my God, the dog is crying." Libby quickly put the statue down and left the room. The casting, she explained later, was inhabited by the spirit of a young woman. Her name was Mary Wood or Woods and because she liked to cook she could often be found in the kitchen. She was very sad, Libby said. What had produced this strange visit from Libby, Victor and Pamela didn't know, and his cousin seemed equally perplexed by her visit. All Libby could say was that it was just something she felt she had to do.

In the face of mounting evidence, Victor's skepticism had all but disappeared. Particularly alarming for Victor, the events seemed personally directed against him. While Pamela had witnessed several strange happenings, most of the activity took place when only Victor was at home. What did Mary — if that was her name — have against him?

For the Oultons, the last straw came several weeks later when Victor was in the kitchen. He had just turned out the light and was preparing to leave when he was suddenly blinded by a flood of intense light. "I thought someone as a gag had flashed a camera," Victor recalled. But when he checked outside the house, there was nobody there. Even more disturbing, a few months earlier Pamela had experienced a similar phenomenon in the same room. It was as if a flash of light had gone off just above eye level, and the incident left her bewildered and frightened.

The next day Victor took out the phone book and looked up "psychics" in the listings. The results weren't favourable; none of those contacted seemed to offer a plausible explanation for what was happening at his home. Later, Pamela's older sister, Debbie, told her that she had found a person who might be able to help. When Victor called John, a Malaysian psychic who had been in Canada only a short time, he was surprised how much John knew about the happenings at his house. However, when John set the price of his services at $200 an hour, Victor felt that the whole thing might have been an elaborate hoax. He refused to pay, but before he could hang up the psychic said, "Wait, I know you have a problem and I have to help you." He agreed not to charge his usual fee.

When John arrived he was accompanied by two Japanese assistants carrying paraphernalia that included a plastic bag full of incense. In order to quiet the spirits, the aromatic amber resin was later placed in pots, lit and carried through the house.

After a few minutes in the house, John offered a description of the man Victor had seen at the top of the stairs, but said this being was not the main spirit-inhabitant of the house. He went on to describe a second entity, a young woman who had been murdered near the house. The incident had taken place many years ago. She had not gone to the light, but remained earth-bound. In recent years she had stayed in a tree on this property until it was cut down, he declared. John then described the ring found in the back yard — it had belonged, he claimed to the dead woman. Victor, who had long ago forgotten about the tree, and said nothing about the ring, was astounded. In the face of such strong evidence, he no longer doubted the psychic's ability.

John examined the house and property, after which he told Victor and Pamela that he didn't like the area where they lived. An Indian massacre had happened not far from where they were, and John believed that that partially explained why their house attracted spirits. Another factor was the appearance of their property, for the Oultons' house had been built on an odd, pie-shaped lot that attracted unhappy spirits. After inspecting the entire dwelling, John told the Oultons to take the mirrors down from their bedroom immediately. "They draw the energy from you when you sleep," he claimed. Similarly, he told Victor and Pamela to take down many of their pictures. In one case a photo of a tiger had to go because the spirit didn't like cats, only dogs. For Victor, who did like cats, this was bad news, as he and Pamela had intended to get a second pet. The good-natured Trina, they believed, would have no difficulty accepting a feline companion.

Before leaving, John asked them to arrange a "gathering" — the psychic didn't like the term séance — to be held at the Oulton house the following week. For the Oultons, who knew little about spiritualism, the notion was unsettling. They are a very private couple, and neither Victor nor Pamela wished it to become generally known that their house was haunted. For this reason they were reluctant to invite neighbours or co-workers to the gathering. Fortunately, a friend of Debbie's was able to find two more couples who were interested in the subject and who could be trusted to keep the matter to themselves. Tom and Margaret were in their late 40s while Danny and Stephanie were a few years younger. Besides these two couples, Victor and Pamela invited Debbie. Thus it was, on a mild March afternoon in 1995, that John and his assistant, Henry, plus five invited guests met the Oultons in their living room.

It had been cloudy all that day and as the cars containing the guests arrived, a light rain was falling. About nine p.m. on March 6, everyone, except John, who stood by the fireplace, made themselves comfortable sitting informally on the sofa and chairs.

John had intended to use Margaret as a channeller, but after almost an hour of futile attempts to put her in a deep trance, he gave up. He then turned his attention to Stephanie. After a few minutes Stephanie appeared to enter a trance state. To demonstrate this John told her to place her arms against her body, and commanded Victor to pull them away from this position. Although Stephanie was only an average-size woman, Victor, who prided himself on his good physical shape, was surprised to discover he couldn't budge either of her arms. (The next day Stephanie would complain about the bruises she received during the test.)

John had put the video camera on the television and turned it to face Stephanie. What emerged during the following hour left Victor and Pamela deeply shaken. Most apparent was the change in Stephanie as John began questioning her. From a mature, outgoing woman, she changed into a different person: her voice rose several octaves and she spoke barely above a whisper. She seemed to shrink into herself and her answers to John's questions were tentative. "I feel cold," she said in a distant voice. "I feel mad, and I'm wet." Under John's questioning she claimed her name was Mary, and she was 20 years old.

What had happened to her, John asked. "I feel like I've been beaten." Under further questioning she would describe the perpetrator as a tall, bearded man in his 40s wearing a checkered shirt, but she could not, or would not, say whether the murderer was known to her. Similarly, she refused to give her full name.

"Do you want me to help you?" John asked.

"I'm all alone. There's no one to help me," she replied. The voice that claimed to be Mary's said she had been "here" about 20 years, although time apparently had little meaning to her since she was not sure of the current year. She said she slept anywhere she could find a warm place. Her favourite places were in the kitchen cupboards and the area under the stairs in the basement.

"I'm also in all the trees," she said.

"Did somebody destroy your house?" John asked.

"I don't know where it went," came the almost inaudible reply.

On further questioning by John, the voice claimed to hold no animosity toward Victor, because he and Pamela were the house owners and belonged there. The same could not be said for the two women who had occupied the basement, for they were intruders.

After about half an hour, John took out a gold wedding band and placed it on the back of Stephanie's hand. "Is this your ring?" he asked.

"No," she said.

He took the band off and replaced it with the ring Victor had found in the back yard, and repeated the question.

"Yes," she replied.

"How do I know this is yours?"

"Because it has three bright lights." As Pamela and Victor observed, Stephanie's eyes had remained closed all this time. And she was correct; there were three diamonds in the setting.

"Do you want it back?"

"No," she said.

John went on to ask her if she wanted justice or peace.

"Peace," came the reply.

Although it had been a relatively balmy evening, the participants noted that the room had become much colder. Shortly after he arrived, John had turned the thermostat up, but it seemed to have made no difference, and several of those present were openly shivering. As soon as John brought Stephanie out of the trance, though, the temperature in living room began to rise.

Following the gathering, the unusual incidents at the Oulton residence decreased. The metallic clang that was heard from the basement, which Victor once believed was the movement of the furnace pipes, has not been heard since. In October, Victor and Pamela felt secure enough to bring a kitten into their home. So far, their pet has made a good adjustment to its new surroundings.

However, strange happenings continue in the house. Although Victor is a meticulous person, many of his CD recordings still disappear without a trace. Unexplained odours persist, but they are now reminiscent more of burnt toast than decay. At night, Trina, continues to refuse to stay on her mat in the hall and the Oultons allow her to sleep in their bedroom where she seems happy.

A study of the history of the Langley area reveals that John was correct: there was an Indian massacre not far from where the Oultons live. In 1837, 600 Yuculta Indians from Quadra Island prepared to attack the village of their traditional enemies, the Quantlans. The Yuculta didn't realize that the Quantlans lived near Fort Langley and were thus considered under Hudson's Bay Company protection. When the Yuculta war canoes rounded a bend in the Fraser, the fort's grapeshot-loaded cannons suddenly opened up, bringing down a deadly rain upon the vessels. Within minutes almost all the canoes were either destroyed or heavily damaged, and the Fraser, it was said, ran red with the blood of the victims. Those attackers who escaped the Hudson's Bay cannons were hunted down by the Quantlans and slaughtered. The battle was a turning point, for the once-powerful Yucultas never fully recovered from this defeat.

The mystery concerning Mary Wood or Woods, though, remains unsolved. Looking back more than 20 years, no person with that name is still listed as missing within British Columbia, and there is no evidence that a woman with that name was murdered in this province during the recent past. Yet it should be noted that during the gathering, Mary was often reluctant to answer personal questions. She clearly did not wish the circumstances surrounding her death to be discussed.

Like other families living in haunted houses, the Oultons are faced with many more questions than answers. The realization that they may have some knowledge of an unsolved murder continues to bother Victor and Pamela. They wonder, given the circumstances surrounding her death, if Mary's spirit can ever find peace. Living in a haunted house has little appeal, but the Oultons are reluctant to consider moving. To allow the ghosts to force them out would be a defeat, and neither Victor nor Pamela is prepared to submit easily.

## HAUNTED BRIARWOOD

When Dennis and Sharon Seymour bought their home a few miles outside Vernon in April 1967, they wanted a house with plenty of room to raise a large family. Indeed Briarwood was spacious; it contained eight bedrooms upstairs, as well as a big kitchen, dining room, living room and music room on the main floor. Yet the house was more crowded than the Seymours knew at first. Briarwood had its own complement of ghosts.

\* \* \* \* \*

Before moving into their new home, the couple spent several weeks cleaning and doing minor repairs. Although the Seymours had not been told the house was haunted when they signed the purchase papers, it did not take them long to notice a number of odd occurrences. The first was the wind — it was certainly more than a draft — that seemed to blow through the house. When they worked downstairs the couple would also hear doors and windows banging shut upstairs. If they happened to be cleaning upstairs, the noises would come from the rooms below them.

Another common and unsettling occurrence was the fact that lights in the rooms would go on and off by themselves. If a light was on when Sharon or Dennis left a room, it would frequently be found switched off when they returned. On other occasions, lights turned off when the couple had gone out would be found burning when they returned.

At first Dennis and Sharon believed these incidents to be the result of natural causes, for the house was then more than 60 years old — it had been built by Archibald Giles, a Vernon businessman, in 1906. However, one day Sharon was standing downstairs, washing a ceiling in a closet, when she suddenly felt something grab her dress and pull with some force. Thinking it was one of her younger children, Sharon said, "Get down and leave me alone." But when she looked at where the child should have been standing, there was no one. Nor could it have been anyone else, for when she checked she discovered all her children playing outside.

Several weeks later, Marisa, the Seymours' eight-year-old daughter, had a frightening encounter in the same room. Sharon was working outside while Dennis had taken a load of trash to the dump. When she couldn't find Marisa playing outside, Sharon was not particularly worried, assuming the little girl had gone with her father to the dump. As she worked, Sharon occasionally heard the sound of sobbing coming from some distance away, but since she believed she was the only one home, she thought little of it. Finally after some time she decided to check inside the house. As she entered the door she heard someone crying. Upon investigating, she found that the sound was coming from the same closet where she had experienced the hard pull on her dress a few weeks earlier. When she opened the door, she saw Marisa huddled in the corner. "Mommy," the child said, "someone pushed me in the closet."

Apparently Marisa had been playing in the room when she was shoved into the closet and the door shut behind her. Left alone in the darkness, the little girl had been very frightened. Sharon examined the closet closely. The door handles were on the outside, so it was impossible for the girl to pull the door shut from the inside.

The Seymours had been in the house about two years when they happened to be at a cocktail party. During the evening Sharon was introduced to the husband of one of Archibald Giles' descendants. After discussing the old house for a few minutes, the man said, "Have you met the ghost yet?" To that point the Seymours had said nothing to friends and neighbours about the strange happenings at Briarwood. Although the man would say nothing more, it was clear to Sharon that their house was haunted.

The comings and goings of the ghost were frequently marked by the opening and closing of bedroom doors. These happenings were so common that the Seymours eventually ignored the sounds. One room, however, seemed to be at the centre of the haunting.

Not long after the Seymour family moved in, Sharon's brother, Dale Weist, came to live with them and was given the master bedroom. Hardly had he settled in when the young man awoke during the night with the feeling that something was pressing his head down on the pillow. The incidents in which he seemed to be held down by some powerful force became so frequent that Dale eventually realized that the only way to have whatever it was leave him alone was to tell it in no uncertain terms to go, and then to pull the bed covers over his head. After that, he was no longer abused by the spirit.

Sharon had another odd experience one night when she had been out and returned home quite late. After getting out of the car, she heard the sound of a deep male voice laughing at her. Since it seemed to be coming from Dale's room she assumed it was her brother. "What the hell are you laughing at," Sharon said, annoyed at such rude behaviour. However, when she entered the house she found her husband and brother fast asleep in front of the fire downstairs. Since there was no other adult male in the house, Sharon was at a loss to explain the occurrence.

About this time Dale moved away, and Dennis and Sharon decided to re-occupy their old room. They had not been there many nights when Sharon was suddenly awakened by a force pressing down on her chest. Whatever it was, it was very powerful. When she tried to call out to Dennis, the pressure on her throat became so great that she couldn't speak. Once, Sharon recalled, "It got so bad, I thought you're not going to do this to me. With all my strength I tried to break away and threw myself over top of my husband and onto the floor." After that, Sharon was no longer troubled by the invisible force.

Over the years, when the Seymours gave up their room to overnight guests, it was common the next morning to hear visitors complain about an invisible weight that seemed to pin them in their bed. They also often remarked on the chill in the master bedroom, although Sharon and Dennis did not, themselves, notice that the room was colder than other parts of the house. One night, one of Sharon's friends was awoken by a male voice calling her name. "Would it have been your ghost?" the woman asked the next morning. Sharon could only answer yes.

The number of unexplained occurrences in that room seemed to decrease, but they never stopped entirely. Several years ago Shawn, one of the Seymours' daughters, met a man overseas and the two were married. When she returned with Donald, her new husband, Dennis and Sharon gave the newlyweds their own bedroom. Shawn, who had grown up with the presence in the house, had not told her husband that the room was haunted, but it did not take him long to discover that something was wrong. During their first night in the room, the young man was awakened by the shaking of the bed. Thinking it must have been his imagination he did not mention it to his wife, but the next night, he experienced the feeling of the heavy weight upon him, and a sensation of choking when he tried to call out. In the morning, when he reported the incident to his mother-in-law, Sharon told him that it was a mistake to give in to the ghost. Instead, he must get angry with it and tell it to leave him alone. The next night when the manifestation returned, he took Sharon's advice with the result that it never troubled him for the remainder of his stay in the Seymour home.

On another occasion, Sharon awoke late at night and saw a small boy standing by her bedside. Although she cannot recall how he was dressed, she remembers him as being about eight or nine years old, with blond hair. Thinking she must be dreaming, she said, "You're not real," and turned away to face the window. Before she closed her eyes again, though, she suddenly saw what appeared to be fireworks on the other side of the bedroom curtain. Seconds later she watched fire appear to erupt in the direction of the house opposite. She arose and awakened the entire household, saying that the house across the street was on fire, but when Dennis pulled back the curtain the dwelling was as dark and quiet as might be expected at that hour.

"You must have been asleep," he said, but Sharon was sure she had been wide awake. After everyone had returned to bed and the lights were extinguished, Sharon turned to face the wall when she was suddenly aware that the little boy was again standing before her.

"I did that on purpose so you wouldn't go back to sleep," he said. He touched Sharon's hand and kissed her on the cheek and said, "Confederation was in 1867."

At that time Sharon had no idea when Canada had become a country. The next day when she looked it up she noted that the proof the boy offered of his visit had been correct: Confederation was indeed in 1867. Yet Sharon had no idea who the child was or why he had chosen such a strange way to make his presence known.

While the sound of phantom footsteps, which are often associated with house hauntings, have only rarely been heard at Briarwood, Sharon notes that common household objects are prone to disappear for months at a time. Usually these items turn up in places the Seymours have previously searched. One of the ghosts has another way of making its presence known. At times it follows her from the main floor up to the attic where it turns on the light for her before she reaches for the wall switch.

Who are the ghosts that haunt Briarwood? About three or four years after moving in, Sharon and Dennis had two friends, Margaret and Ken, who were attending university in Vancouver, arrive as guests. Given the strange goings-on in the house, the four young people thought it would be interesting to see if they could contact the otherworldly inhabitants of Briarwood. Although they had never used it, the Seymours had earlier acquired a Ouija board. The couples had hardly placed the board on the table and allowed their fingers to lightly touch the surface of the heart-shaped planchette when the object began moving rapidly. For the three days their friends remained as guests, the Ouija was the centre of interest.

The first entity to announce itself claimed to be Archibald Giles, the first owner of Briarwood. Giles appeared to be rather a fussy sort of person, somewhat put out that the Seymours had turned his den into a utility room. He also objected to the colour of the house, claiming that it should be repainted grey with black trim.

After a few hours, a second entity challenged Giles for control of the board. It claimed its name was Peter Gates, and that it had lived on the land before Giles had acquired the property. Gates seemed thoroughly evil.

*Briarwood, built in 1906 by Vernon businessman Archibald Giles.* (PHOTO BY THE AUTHOR)

One of the questions the couples put to Gates was whether it was he who pushed Marisa into the closet.

The planchette moved to "YES" in the top left corner of the board.

"Why?" Sharon asked.

"I WANT HER," the pointer spelled out.

"Why?" they said.

"BECAUSE SHE IS MY WIFE."

"How are you going to get her?"

"KILL," it spelled out.

The entity calling itself Peter Gates went on to claim that Marisa's real name was Beth, and to predict even the date of the little girl's death a few years hence. The board had become something more than an object of harmless curiosity; there was something sinister controlling the planchette. Naturally, Sharon and Dennis were very upset. After their friends had returned to university, Sharon received a letter from Margaret who had done some research into Ouija boards. Everything she was able to discover, her friend said, indicated that these boards were bad. "Get rid of it, burn the thing," Margaret wrote.

A distraught Sharon eventually confided Peter Gates' dire threat to her mother who said, "Don't worry about it. The supernatural can't hurt you if you don't let it." It was nevertheless a great relief when the date predicted by Peter Gates came and went, and Marisa remained as happy and healthy as ever. Today Marisa is married with four children of her own.

As the years passed, the ghosts haunting Briarwood have become less active. Sharon, on occasion, is still surprised when on entering a dark room, the light bulb turns on before she has the chance to reach for the switch. Yet in this case the unseen entity is simply being helpful.

## THE NEIGHBOUR

The house Lorne and Audrey Briere purchased in Port Coquitlam was not haunted by a previous resident of the dwelling. The ghost, instead, was that of a former next-door neighbour.

\* \* \* \* \*

Soon after the Brieres moved into their house on a quiet residential street in Port Coquitlam, they met Frank, their elderly, next-door neighbour who had been a long-time resident of the block. For many years Frank had shared the house with his brother, Clarence, who had died only a few months before the Brieres arrived in 1979.

The loss of his brother had been a severe blow to Frank, who was in ill health himself. Frank, though, continued to manage on his own with the aid of his nephew, Bob, who often came over to help. The Brieres gradually became well acquainted with Frank who would often speak of his recently deceased brother. Clarence, Frank explained, had been a frequent visitor to Lorne and Audrey's house, for he had struck up a strong friendship with the previous owner of the property.

The Brieres were pleased with their new residence, which seemed to have a warm, homey atmosphere. This was true everywhere except in one room: the bedroom they had designated for storage. Lorne and Audrey soon discovered that it was an area they preferred to avoid. One reason was that it was always cold.

34

While it could be warm in every other part of the house, a chill hung in the air there. Also, an odour of something rotten could often be detected. The smell was not overpowering, but remained nonetheless unpleasant.

Although perplexed by the origin of the odours and the chill, Lorne and Audrey assumed that there had to be a rational explanation for the phenomena. Since no one had to stay there long, the unpleasantness could be tolerated for short periods. Yet, as time passed, the couple found more evidence that there was something deeply disturbing about this spot. In time, the couple noticed that while the two family cats made free use of the rest of the house, they never entered the storage room. For both pets, even to pass the open door sometimes produced a strange reaction: their fur stood on end and they would howl pitifully.

As they settled in, Lorne and Audrey experienced other strange occurrences. Doors would slam and lights in various rooms turned on and off by themselves, dishes in the cupboard rattled and household items would inexplicably go missing. The disappearance of keys, tools, and other objects seemed particularly aimed at Lorne. At times, Lorne and Audrey would hear various thumps and bumps that originated elsewhere in the house. No matter how hard they tried, they could never find the source of these happenings.

The only explanation seemed to be that their house was haunted. Given that they were unaware of anyone dying in the house, the Brieres suspected that their ghost might be Clarence, the former next-door neighbour. Before he became sick he had spent much time in their home, and he might now wander beyond the boundaries of his own property to visit their dwelling.

The Brieres had been in the house several years when Frank became so ill he could no longer manage on his own. He was placed in a nursing home where he died a few weeks later. The elderly man had bequeathed his house to his nephew Bob. Bob's attempts to rent the dwelling were not successful, however, for the tenant moved out after only a few months. In case there were any problems while it remained empty, Bob gave a set of house keys to Lorne and Audrey.

During this time the Brieres had a visit from Linda, an out-of-town friend. One night while she had gone out to the side of the house to bring in an armload of firewood, she happened to look at the house next door. Standing at the window was a frail-looking older man wearing a checked shirt. After returning inside, she mentioned to Lorne that she thought the house next door was supposed to be vacant, and went on to describe what she had seen. Lorne at first didn't believe Linda. He took her next door and showed her that because a refrigerator had been moved next to the window, it was impossible to have seen anyone there. Moreover, Linda's description of the man fit no one with whom Lorne was familiar. Linda, however, steadfastly maintained that she had seen an elderly man next door.

To settle the matter, Lorne phoned Bob and provided him with a description of the intruder. "You just described Uncle Clarence to a tee," said the shocked voice on the other end of the line. The incident left Bob so upset that he refused to enter the house again.

Although the ghost was never seen again, the disturbances at the Briere home continued until the sudden death of Bob the following year. Much to the relief of Lorne and Audrey, the haunting of their home suddenly stopped. Gradually the unpleasant atmosphere that had long hung over the storage area seemed to disappear. His nephew's death seemed to break Clarence's tie to the earthly plane, a connection that had endured beyond the grave.

## THE MAN IN THE PLAID SHIRT

In 1977, Heather Grassick and two women friends shared a house in Westbank, across Okanagan Lake narrows from Kelowna. From the time they moved in, there seemed to be something eerie about the place. All three women experienced a feeling of vague discomfort, particularly at night. It was as though they were not alone; someone was watching them. When she was alone at night, Heather would sometimes hear the measured sound of breathing, as if someone was in the room with her. There were also noises in the attic: the women would frequently hear what sounded like furniture being shuffled around upstairs. When they went to the attic to investigate, nothing ever appeared to have been moved.

The beach-front property made it ideal for enjoying the pleasures of a warm Interior summer. The side of the single-storey house that faced the lake had many windows that provided a excellent view of the water. One day Heather and her roommates invited some friends over to the house, and after spending some time inside, they decided to move to the beach where they could enjoy the evening breeze blowing in from the lake. While the young people were sitting on the shore, one woman happened to glance back toward the house, where the room lights had been left on. "Who's in the house?" she said.

The others looked around and counted heads. Everyone was there, and no one should have been in the dwelling.

"Well, I just saw a guy in a plaid shirt walk through the kitchen."

A thorough search of the house was made, but it turned up no one. Some months later, though, the renters where talking to the woman who owned the property. She had lived there for some time with her husband until he died several years earlier.

"Did he have a favourite kind of shirt he usually wore?" one of the renters asked.

"Why yes," the older woman answered, obviously surprised at the question. "Plaid."

## THE CHOKING MAN

According to most witnesses, apparitions are more than simple "tape recordings" playing back past events. In the case of Salt Spring Island's choking man, though, it seems that no conscious entity was associated with the occurrence. Rather, it was no more than a replay of a violent incident that had taken place years earlier.

\* \* \* \* \*

Within easy reach of Victoria, Salt Spring Island was the first of the Gulf Island chain to support large-scale European settlement. As early as 1859, a group of destitute Australian prospectors had moved to Salt Spring to become homesteaders. These hardy pioneers were followed by other new arrivals including a number of free blacks who had moved north from California.

One of the early European settlers was Adolphus Treage who, in 1862, took up property at the south end of the island. As Treage prospered, his original house became inadequate, and he built a new residence a short distance away. The old dwelling became accommodation for those needing temporary shelter.

On one occasion a violent incident took place at the old homestead: a man's throat was cut. Although the details have been lost to history, a record of the grisly deed remained. The house gradually developed a reputation for being haunted, and after a woman visitor claimed to have been forcibly grabbed by the shoulders, Island people avoided it.

Some time after the turn of the century, the 600-acre property was purchased by the Fraser family, who ran sheep and cattle there. The Frasers soon built their own house, but the old Treage buildings remained. By now, though, the first house had fallen into disrepair. The paint had worn so completely off the exterior that it was impossible to say what colour it had been. Inside, the air was heavy with the smell of decay.

During the heat of summer, the dilapidated dwelling did have an occasional tenant. Don, one of the Fraser children, would sometimes spend a night alone in the cool old house. Although the old place was certainly eerie, he found nothing disturbing there — nothing that is, except a strange noise that seemed to begin somewhere within the dwelling. To Don it sounded like a calf after its throat had been cut: a terrible "a-hough" noise. It was quite faint at first, but gradually became louder.

The sound was thought to have been made by a draft that took on a throaty noise as it channelled through the walls, but search as they might, the family couldn't find the source of the disturbance. It was impossible to say from where the sound came; it seemed rather to be part of the atmosphere of the house. The eerie choking noise was not only a night-time phenomenon; it was also heard during the daylight hours. The Fraser children became so used to the presence that they would take friends there with the purpose of frightening them.

Eventually the old house was torn down and, as might be expected, the ghastly noises stopped. However, for those who heard the sound of the choking man, the incident remained a vivid memory. When Don Fraser recalled the incidents years later, he had little doubt that the source of the sound was something unnatural — something very unnatural, indeed.

## Do Not Disturb

Many people first encounter a ghost when they start making alterations to their home. It isn't certain why this is the case, but some researchers have speculated that ghosts are really forms of energy recorded in the wood and stone of a dwelling, and changes to a building sometimes put the "recorder" in playback mode. Past events are thus heard or seen in the present. Other theorists believe that ghosts are innately conservative beings who abhor change. As a result, they come back to express their displeasure when remodelling is begun.

\* \* \* \* \*

When Anne Edwards and her husband Randy bought their two-storey home on Lorne Avenue in Maple Ridge 20 years ago, the structure had not been well maintained. Originally built as a farmhouse in the 1930s, the property had been subdivided among the children of the original occupants. As the years passed, the aging parents found it increasingly difficult to maintain the building. After the father's death, the dilapidated home was placed on the market in the mid-1970s, and purchased by a couple who intended to make a few alterations and then quickly turn the property over. One afternoon the woman and one of her friends arrived to begin a major cleaning. They were intending to stay overnight and the owner had brought her dog, a Dalmatian, with her. They had not even stepped on the back stairs when the dog's fur stood on end and it uttered a low howl. No matter how firmly they tried, the women could not coax the animal to come inside.

They had been cleaning only a short time when they suddenly became very cold, and the two began to shiver. Unnerved, the women decided to sleep, not in the house as they had planned, but in the car. The next day they quickly finished the work and left. Rather than completing the alterations, the husband and wife immediately put the dwelling on the market.

The new owner made some repairs but didn't remain there long, and in the late fall of 1978, Anne and Randy purchased the property and moved in. Rather than turning a quick profit, the couple wished to make the dwelling their permanent residence. The house, though, required much more work. The master bedroom, which was on the main floor, was too small to accommodate the couple's waterbed, and Randy found it necessary to rip out a wall to expand their sleeping area.

Soon after the work was begun, Anne was in the kitchen speaking on the telephone when the wall clock suddenly flew past her shoulder and crashed to the floor. The clock could not have fallen from the wall; it was hooked securely in place and connected to the nearby outlet by an electrical cord that passed through one of the kitchen cupboards. Yet the instrument with its attached cord had crossed the width of the room before landing at her feet.

When Randy returned from work, Anne explained what had happened, and told him that she believed their new house was haunted. A long-time skeptic, he failed to believe his wife, and instead challenged the ghost to make itself known. Suddenly, a large metal pot, which had been standing with the dishes on the drain board by the sink, slowly lifted up, moved across the room to where Randy was standing and clattered to his feet. The incident changed his view of ghosts.

A few days later, the couple purchased a new clock for the kitchen, this time a battery-operated model. The clock had not been in place long when it came off the wall, flew across the room, and hit Anne on her shoulder. She picked it up and examined it carefully. Since it wasn't broken she returned it to the wall. "That's enough of this stuff," she said to the ghost, but three days later she was in the kitchen again when the clock lifted from the wall and struck her. Angrily Anne demanded that the ghost leave the clock alone, and that if it removed the object from the wall once more, she would not hang it up again. After that, the clock remained in place.

The ghost found other ways to make its presence known. When Randy was scheduled to work night shift, Anne was alone in the house. She would retire to bed, only to be disturbed by the sound of footsteps pacing back and forth in one of the upstairs bedrooms. Sometimes she would become so frustrated by the noise that she would go upstairs and tell the phantom visitor to be quiet.

On one occasion she was alone watching television when she was bothered by measured footsteps coming from the room above her head. Angrily, she went upstairs and demanded that the ghost stop its behaviour. When she returned downstairs, the footsteps were replaced by an even more disturbing cacophony. It was as if someone was using the room as a bowling lane, for she could hear a heavy ball rolling along a wooden floor. When she examined the room in the morning, she discovered nothing that could account for the sound.

Although she never saw anyone during the most active time of the haunting, Anne often had the feeling that she was being watched. The phantom, Anne believes, is a man, for one day she and her daughter were the only adults in the house when Chad, her young grandson, came running from the playroom, yelling, "Man there! Man there!" When the child calmed down he told his mother and grandmother that a man had told him to turn the television off. "No way could we make him go back there, he was so scared," Anne remembered.

The disturbances have not been confined to the Edwards' home. One neighbour reported seeing a shadow pass across his recreation room bar, followed by the tinkle of glasses. The mobility of the ghost may not be surprising, since that entire block once belonged to one family. The ghost may haunt the land that he once owned.

After the Edwards completed the major renovations to the house in 1994, the noises stopped. Although the ghost is quiet now, they have no doubt that the whine of a saw or the pound of a hammer would bring back their phantom visitor.

* * * * *

Home is the focal point of the lives of most men and women, so it is not unusual that presences often inhabit these places. Yet it is also true that while houses are the most common of the haunted venues, supernatural beings are frequently found elsewhere. Theatres, hotels, pubs, roads, or just about anywhere can be the haunt of ghosts.

CHAPTER THREE

# Haunted Theatres

A theatre can be a scary place when the audience, cast and crew have left. The sound of a dripping faucet or running toilet that was scarcely heard an hour earlier can become so loud as to seem to shake the building, and once-innocent shadows appear to take on a life of their own. Yet it would be a mistake to dismiss all theatre happenings as the result of overactive imaginations. Ghostly activity over the years is frequently seen, heard or felt not by one or two individuals, but by many people.

## THE VOGUE THEATRE

Vancouver's Vogue Theatre, at 918 Granville Street, does not seem a place that would attract ghosts. Yet, for some reason, this relatively modern-looking facility has far more than its share of strange happenings. Why the Vogue is a magnet for paranormal occurrences remains a mystery, but it is arguably one of the most haunted buildings in British Columbia.

\* \* \* \* \*

Unlike most haunted theatres which have had a long history of stage productions, the Vogue, until recently, was used almost exclusively as a movie house. It was built with dressing rooms to accommodate a large number of vaudeville performers, but the space was almost never used for that purpose. The building was leased before it was completed to the Toronto-based Odeon theatre chain. Paul L. Nathanson, the forward-looking president of that group, thought live stage performances were outdated: the way to fill theatre seats was to show moving pictures. Thus it was that on April 15, 1941, the theatre's first-night gala featured not a stage production, but the movie, *I See Ice*, starring the British comic actor, George Formby. Because Canada and Britain were at war with the Axis states, Formby donated an autographed guitar to be auctioned in aid of a fund for victims of London air raids.

As theatres go, the Vogue was something special. Although not the biggest, in 1941 the theatre could claim to be the most up-to-date in the city. The modernistic art deco façade, complete with a 63-foot-high sign adorned by a ten-foot-tall figure of Diana, the Roman goddess of the moon, made it a favourite among sophisticated

*The Vogue Theatre in Vancouver.* (COURTESY OF DIANE BELYK)

43

Vancouverites. The theatre's state-of-the-art air conditioner and the most modern projection and amplifying systems in the city were an added bonus. For years the Vogue was the flagship of Odeon's British Columbia operation.

Time, however, does not stand still and by the mid-1960s, Vancouver was changing. As many of the city's more fashionable enterprises closed their doors and moved elsewhere, the three great queens of Vancouver's Theatre Row, the Orpheum, the Capitol and the Vogue, now surveyed a realm of grimy cafes, shabby book stores, and dimly lit pawn shops. Despite several attempts to revitalize what had long been regarded as Vancouver's cultural heartland, conditions didn't improve, and those theatre-goers who ventured downtown had to share the sidewalk with prostitutes, petty thieves and beggars who were now the common currency of this neighbourhood. In 1967, the Vogue received its last major face-lift. After that, the once-proud queen of Granville Street began to wear the same weather-beaten expression as its block neighbours.

The fortunes of the Vogue reached their low point in 1987 when its doors closed as a first-run movie house. The building remained shut until 1991, when it was reopened, this time mainly as a venue for live performances. Fifty years after its construction, the theatre was at last serving the purpose for which it had been built. It did not take the new staff long, though, to notice strange happenings. One morning, several posters that had been piled on a storage area shelf at lock-up the previous night were found spread neatly on the floor. Ominously, house staff reported what sounded like chains being dropped on a wooden floor. Also, unexplained thumping and bumping noises were often heard during times when no one should have been in the performance area. In the basement, heavy fire doors with spring closures were seen to open and shut on their own.

An eerie-looking narrow corridor, which extends the length of the basement, has been the site of many unusual occurrences. Off this passageway open a number of small, airless cubicles that are used as service shops and dressing rooms. Ken St. Pierre, the theatre's former technical director had one odd experience when he was alone in the basement. As he moved along the corridor he felt something pass him, brushing his body. Startled, he turned

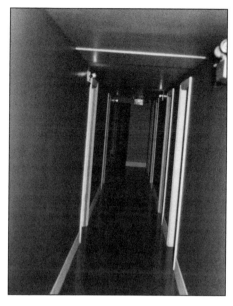

*The narrow hallway under the stage in the Vogue Theatre, which has been the site of many unusual happenings.* (PHOTO BY THE AUTHOR)

around in time to catch a shadow out of the corner of his eye. What it was he couldn't say. The basement is a weird place, according to St. Pierre. "I don't like staying there alone."

When Bill Allman began working for the Vogue Theatre in May, 1994, he heard some of these accounts, but given that such stories are a common part of theatre lore, he didn't put much stock in them. Less than a month later, however, Allman experienced something that was to change his mind. As operations manager he spent many hours in the basement of the theatre. Late one night he was the last staff member in the building. Attending to a few details before finally locking up, he went down the stairs behind the stage into the basement. As he recalled later:

> I was putting something away in a cabinet in the carpentry room and was overcome by the feeling that there was someone behind me — that feeling when someone is just about to grab you. I wheeled around and caught a shadowy impression of someone sailing by the door.

The following month, a friend of one of the staff members witnessed an apparition in the projection booth. The experience so frightened her that she refused to discuss what she had seen. In August, Bill Allman had a second encounter with the unexplained. It was in the daytime, at an hour when only Allman and theatre manager, "Rockin" Norton, were in the theatre. While Allman made preparations for the evening's performance, Norton remained upstairs in his office. The theatre had been putting on a tribute to the Beatles, and a set of drums, similar to the kind once used by Ringo Starr, was left on stage. Allman explained:

As I was walking under the stage through the [basement] hallway, I heard a very distinct pattern being played on the drums — a boom, boom, boom, with a little cymbal shot. I came upstairs onto the stage, and [as] soon as I rounded the corner the drumming stopped. The sticks were sitting on the kit at the time. There was no one in the house, there was no one on the stage, and the only way that someone could have got [away] would have been to go up the central aisle of the theatre or else to walk over top of me and come down the stairs.

Immediately following the incident, Allman went upstairs to find Norton sitting at his desk. With only the two men in the theatre at the time, the drum solo defied normal explanation. Later that evening, the phantom drummer was heard again, this time by one of the stage carpenters as he was locking up the theatre. Again, no one was in the vicinity of the drum kit when the incident occurred.

During the following months, unusual activity at the Vogue decreased; however, those who believed that the ghost may have gone elsewhere were to be disappointed. On November 1, 1995, *Unforgettable: The Music of Nat King Cole*, starring Montreal jazz singer Densil Pinnock opened a two-month run at the Vogue. One member of the supporting cast was the well-known Canadian performer, Shane McPherson. While McPherson had heard many stories of theatre ghosts at other houses during his 20-year stage career, he had always been skeptical of such tales. During rehearsals, he had heard strange noises at the Vogue — the sound of what appeared to be cloth rubbing together — but concluded it had to be just his imagination. Until the evening performance on November 14, he believed he had never personally encountered the supernatural. Then, during what had been a routine performance in his role as jazz great, Mel Torme, everything changed.

The cast was performing the "Route 66" dance number in which McPherson had to do a particularly demanding tap solo. The dancer faced the difficult task of concentrating on the steps while at the same time making the piece look easy and enjoyable to the audience. As he danced, McPherson looked toward the audience, and when he turned toward stage left he saw a man standing under the exit sign by the front row. The form was solid, so solid in fact that the performer was sure he was a living person. The man appeared to be in his mid-30s with close-cropped dark hair. He was quite tall, with a narrow face, and was wearing a long, cream-coloured dinner jacket. What struck McPherson as surprising was that the man's body was turned toward the stage with his right hand extended behind him as though he had just closed the exit door, something that would not ordinarily have been done in the middle of a performance. (As McPherson discovered later, the door was not directly under the exit sign as he had believed, but some distance away down a long hall.) As the dancer continued to watch, the man looked up at him, making eye contact but with a blank expression on his face. Then he was gone. "The only way I can describe it," McPherson said later, "is as television would do a fade-out, this individual dissolved. He simply dissolved in front of my eyes."

With his mouth open in astonishment, McPherson lost all track of where he was. He ended the number early. At intermission, he questioned the staff about whether they had seen anything unusual during his solo, but no one admitted anything. This was not entirely surprising since at that moment the eyes of everyone in the theatre were focussed on the dancer. Only McPherson would have been looking toward the exit door. It was at this time that he was informed that strange occurrences were not uncommon at the Vogue. "That [incident] was not my imagination," McPherson affirmed later. "I saw that individual that night. I'll swear to that."

The following day David Raun, a technician, also had an encounter with the phantom. As he was preparing to lock up the theatre following the afternoon matinée, he walked to the area in front of the stage and looked up toward the projection booth. He saw someone standing in the doorway. Although the body appeared to be in shadows, the face was clear. The clean-shaven man had short hair and chiselled features with dark eyebrows. Like McPherson a day earlier, Raun hardly saw the apparition before it faded away. The technician quickly ran up the stairs to the projection booth, but there was no sign of an intruder. Shaken, Raun locked up and went to the brightly lit cafe next door to seek out his friends. It was some time before he felt comfortable about being alone in the building.

Not until several days later did Raun hear of McPherson's experience with the ghost. As they compared notes, the men were struck by the similarity between what they had seen. The only important difference seemed to be that in Raun's sighting, the individual's body was not distinct.

A few months earlier, Raun had had a strange experience in the theatre. During the summer, he had been working on a catwalk that ran above the stage. It was here that technicians could gain access to the cables connecting the spotlights to the control board at the rear of the theatre. Given that they were in the upper reaches of the building and it was during the full heat of summer, the catwalks tended to be extremely uncomfortable places to work. Raun had hauled the cables up a ladder and was laying them along the catwalk. He was concentrating on the task at hand when he suddenly felt something brush his right shoulder and pass behind his back. The feeling was so strong that he was sure one of the technicians had pushed past him. At the same time the air suddenly became cold and Raun shivered involuntarily. He looked up, expecting to see someone walking along the catwalk, but no one was there. It was as if whoever brushed passed him had suddenly vanished.

In the summer of 1996, Stephanie, one of the box-office workers, had her own experience with the phantom of the Vogue. She was alone in the lobby one afternoon when she suddenly sensed a presence. At first she thought she had seen movement from the street reflected in one of the lobby mirrors, but as she turned around she caught a glimpse of a shape climbing the balcony stairs. She saw the image only for a second before it disappeared around a corner, but she had no doubt that someone or something had been there.

The phantom of the Vogue seems to have little trouble materializing. To date, since the Vogue reopened in 1991, the spectre has been seen by at least six people on at least seven different occasions. Yet the haunting may have begun much earlier. There is some evidence that the ghost has been attached to the theatre for many years. During the time when the Vogue operated as a motion-picture theatre, concession workers reported seeing a spectre in a long coat haunting the building. Ghost tales, though, were not popular with Odeon management who may have felt that his presence would have adversely affected attendance. Staff members were encouraged to keep such stories to themselves.

It seems unlikely that the presence could have been a stage performer. During the years, live acts were sometimes added to the theatre's movie bill, but they were the exception rather than the rule. Also, it is doubtful that anyone associated with the live stage could have formed a strong enough attachment to the Vogue to want to return there after death. What appears more likely is that the apparition was a member of the theatre staff during the period when the Vogue's star was at its height — someone who didn't wish to give up the glamour of the entertainment business. The identity of the phantom of the Vogue, though, remains anyone's guess.

A footnote to the Vogue theatre haunting: On the night of Friday, June 6, 1997, the last performance of *Gabereau,* the popular CBC radio program hosted by Vicki Gabereau, was taped before a sold-out audience at the Vogue Theatre. Gabereau began the program by presenting a brief account of the theatre's history and her connection to the cinema during her childhood.

"This theatre is haunted by a ghost," she noted flatly, and described the man in the cream-coloured dinner jacket.

She quickly went on to other topics that did not include the resident phantom. Later, in the middle of Gabereau's interview with actor Jackson Davies, an ear-piercing squeal erupted from the house speakers. The technicians quickly went to work on the problem and the noise ceased, but a few minutes later the cacophony arose again, forcing the staff to temporarily stop the taping.

While the problem was later described as a case of electronic cross-over in the audio system, there were some in audience who regarded this explanation as too prosaic. They believed that Vicki had earlier evoked the ghost and now he was using the speakers to let everyone know he was there.

## THE MCPHERSON PLAYHOUSE

The modern-looking exterior of Victoria's McPherson Playhouse — the result of a 1960s face lift — belies the theatre's real age. The building was opened shortly before the First World War as a vaudeville house. Over the years, theatre staff have reported that two different ghosts haunt the premises.

* * * * *

According to current technical director Larry Eastick, the theatre, located on Centennial Square in downtown Victoria, has had a difficult history. With the introduction of sound films in the late 1920s, vaudeville began a slow decline, and while the theatre sometimes showed moving pictures, the McPherson never became a successful cinematic venue. Throughout the Depression and the following decade, a number of attempts were made to keep the theatre open, but all met with failure. In the 1950s, a Vancouver theatre company reached an agreement with owner Thomas Shanks McPherson to use the house for productions brought over from the mainland. However, this plan, like so many others, failed after a few seasons and the building was boarded up again. In the late 1960s, as a result of McPherson's will, the theatre passed to the City of Victoria, and after being completely renovated inside and out, became a venue for live theatre. The municipal government, though, had little experience running a civic theatre, and in 1977, the McPherson Foundation took over operation of the building. The site was by then home to the Victoria-based Bastion Theatre Company, which produced a wide range of stage plays.

There are two stories of violent death connected with the McPherson. It is said that some time in the 1920s a theatre manager late one night went up to the second-floor balcony, tied

*The McPherson Playhouse in Victoria.* (PHOTO BY THE AUTHOR)

one end of a rope to the dress circle rail and the other around his neck, and then jumped over the edge. When the stage crew arrived the next day they discovered the man's body hanging above the main floor seats. A decade later, it was rumoured that the closed theatre was sometimes used as an illegal gambling den. According to theatre lore, during one such poker game a man was shot. Immediately all the players vacated the place, leaving the victim to crawl to the street, where his body was later discovered.

One of Eastick's first ghost experiences occurred in the early 1970s during a Bastion Theatre production. After play rehearsals it was common practice for the set and costume designers as well as department heads to meet after everyone else connected with the production had gone home. The purpose of these sessions, which were held in the green room directly under the stage, was to correct any difficulties the senior staff had identified. During one such meeting, Eastick and seven of his colleagues were discussing the rehearsal when suddenly they were aware of the sound of heavy footsteps crossing the stage above them. Because all the remaining cast and crew had been sent home, the only logical conclusion was that there was an intruder in the building. The staff exited the green room, split into three groups, and ran immediately on stage, taking the stairs to the left and right, as well as from the orchestra pit. Since the searchers acted quickly, an individual would have had no time to escape. Yet as Eastick recalled, no one was found.

Some months later, Eastick and another staff member were alone in the building. They were working downstairs when they heard a distinctive heavy tread walking across the stage above their heads. Again, a search of the theatre was made, and it failed to reveal an intruder.

In 1990, one of the custodians approached Eastick, considerably upset, and reported seeing one of the heavy cables used to control the props oscillating at a high rate. It was particularly interesting because this cable was one of eight that were connected at the opposite end to a counterweight. If the weight had been disturbed, all the cables should have moved together: it seemed impossible that only one of the braided-steel lines had moved on its own. Although it was suggested that a rat might have scurried up one of the cables, one small rodent could not have produced this effect.

Several years later, another staff member had an encounter with the ghost. During one of the smaller productions, Mary Cavanagh, who was then stage manager of the Bastion Theatre, decided to give direction from the closed balcony. From that location Cavanagh had a better view of the play, and thus it remained only for the technical staff to connect her via a headset and a microphone to the crew backstage. About half way through the first act, Cavanagh said through her microphone, "There's somebody sitting behind me."

"The balcony's supposed to be closed," someone backstage said. "Who's behind you?"

"It's a guy wearing a tux," she said. "He is sitting on the seat back two rows behind, looking down and smiling at me." Assistant technical director Tom Heemskerk paged the front of the house and requested that the theatre manager, Jason Campbell, investigate immediately.

"Is he still there?" Heemskerk said to Cavanagh over the headphones.

"Yes, he's sitting right behind me." No sooner had she spoken than the manager came through the balcony door. Cavanagh turned to point to the intruder, but to her amazement the person had vanished.

While the unidentified male ghost appears to be a fixture at the McPherson, there is also another entity present: she is the Lady in Grey. She wears a high-necked, hoop dress of a style popular many years before the theatre was built. Like her male counterpart, she is almost always seen rather than heard, and often appears to float above the floor.

Although many of the details concerning earlier sightings of her have been lost, it would seem that she has been making her appearances at the theatre for many years. On one occasion in the 1970s, a young actor delivered his lines and exited the stage, waiting in the dark for his cue to return. For some reason he happened to look up to the grid, the area above the stage where the lights are fixed. To his astonishment he saw a billowing grey dress floating from one side of the stage to the other. Before he could alert anyone else, the shape faded away.

Probably none of the earlier sightings, though, were quite as dramatic as the Lady's appearance during rehearsals for a play about a ghost. In the early 1990s, the local theatre company was presenting a play called *Woman in Black*. Everyone connected with the production agreed that it was an excellent script and, because it was set in a haunted theatre, a particularly apt story. "We do a lot of shows," recalled assistant technical director Blair Morris, "but this one was particularly terrifying."

For the cast and crew, *Woman in Black* was difficult to produce because many of the scenes required the actors to move during blackout when all the stage lights were turned off. In the dark, an extra step might mean that a cast member would tumble into the orchestra pit. To prevent distractions, the two lead actors asked that the dress rehearsals be closed — no one was allowed to view the play from the auditorium. However, when the cast moved downstairs to the green room for their break, one of the men was visibly upset. "We specifically asked that there be nobody in the theatre," the actor exclaimed, "and there was this woman — she's all over the balcony."

"Everywhere," the other lead actor confirmed. "She was just walking constantly [and]... at one point she was running in the balcony." After Morris got over his initial shock, he told the two men the story of the Lady in Grey. Everyone returned to the auditorium immediately to see who was in the balcony, but all the seats were empty.

Many of the people connected with the McPherson Playhouse believe that the female ghost is a hold-over from a former building on the site — the Lady in Grey's attire clearly predates the theatre. But the dress could also have been a costume worn by one of the vaudeville performers during the early days. Another possibility is that the Lady may have wandered a few blocks from the location of Victoria's first cemetery on the corner of Douglas and Johnson streets. While most of the bodies were moved from that site in 1860 to the Quadra Street Cemetery, apparently many remains were missed. Like other pioneer communities of the period, Victoria gave little thought to the proper interment of its dead. As to the identity of the man, he may be either the suicidal theatre manager or the murdered gambler, if these stories are true. The ghost's formal attire could be in keeping with the occupation of either individual.

Although the identity of the ghosts isn't known positively, they appear to be benign. Standing in the middle of the stage facing an empty house, many of the production people are awed by a feeling of solemnity, as if they were alone in a great cathedral. Stagehands and technicians also claim that this is in stark contrast to the atmosphere of the McPherson's sister theatre, the Royal, only a few blocks away.

## THE ROYAL THEATRE

The ghost of Victoria's Royal Theatre is rarely seen and only occasionally heard, but it is nonetheless a pervasive presence. According to theatre employees, it is not a good idea to be the last person in the building once the sun has set. Late at night, when most of the performers and crew have gone home, the atmosphere on stage can become so thick that it seems almost solid.

\* \* \* \* \*

The Royal Theatre was constructed as a vaudeville house in 1913, during one of the greatest building booms Victoria ever enjoyed. The stage, which some claimed was the largest west of Chicago, was 40 feet wide and more than 30 feet deep. During its long and colourful history, performers as diverse as Sarah Bernhardt and Tom Jones have brought audiences to their feet.

Yet the Royal also has had a difficult past. Even before the first shot in the First World War was fired, Victoria's balloon of prosperity suddenly collapsed. The Royal struggled through the Depression and the Second World War to be eventually purchased by the Famous Players theatre chain. As a purveyor of "movies for the masses," Victoria's most ornate theatre was given an extensive refitting; many of the original expensive fixtures were removed and replaced by a less ostentatious decor. However, by 1967, the era of the big motion-picture house was over as smaller suburban cinemas were attracting most of the movie-going public. It seemed only a matter of time before the historic Royal Theatre fell under the weight of the wrecking ball. Fortunately, it was saved in 1973 when the municipalities of Victoria, Oak Bay and Saanich

*The Royal Theatre in Victoria.* (PHOTO BY THE AUTHOR)

purchased the structure. The building was gradually refurbished and the lobby, which was small by today's standards, was enlarged. In 1982 the Royal came under the management of the McPherson Foundation which was operating Victoria's other major live theatre. The two buildings share many of the same staff.

Assistant technical director Blair Morris still vividly remembers his first experience alone in the Royal. During one week in 1988 both theatres featured big productions, and without sufficient staff to cover both places, management drafted Morris at the last minute to handle the performance of the Welsh Men's Choir at the Royal. As he recalled later:

> At the end of the night, I knew nothing about the building, I had a list of stuff that I'd written down that I had to check and I was very thorough. They [the choir] had been gone 20 minutes at least out of the building. I'd locked all the doors and started my trip through downstairs checking dressing rooms and turning out lights. I'd come back up [on stage] and discovered I'd made the crucial error of turning out the house lights before I went downstairs. I got to centre stage and I swear . . . it felt like someone took a knife, like a hunting knife, flipped it over and just rammed the point down my back.

Morris wasted no time setting the burglar alarm and vacating the building. The next day he went to return the keys to Larry Eastick at the McPherson. During their meeting, Morris described to Eastick what had happened the previous night.

"Ah," he said, "I see you've met our friend." Eastick went on to explain that many other staff over the years had experienced the same feeling.

Assistant technical director Tom Heemskerk recalled that when he and Morris first worked together at the Royal, they quickly established a routine. If the performance ended before closing time at the neighbourhood pub, one of the men would lock up the theatre while the other went up the street and ordered a glass of beer for his friend. When it was Heemskerk's turn to lock up, he noted that he was greatly discomfited by his final walk across the stage. He found it impossible to look out into the empty house. "There was nothing to see," he said, "but you had the feeling you were very, very unwelcome." When he discussed this with Morris, he discovered that his friend experienced the same feelings during the nights when he was the last person to leave the building. Eventually the two technicians changed their routine so that they both remained in the building during lock up, and the walk across the stage was done together.

Heemskerk and Morris were usually the last staff to leave the building, so not all the crew experienced the entity's full presence. Some staff even claimed that the ghost was only a product of over-active imaginations. However, when the two men offered to pay $50 to anyone who would remain alone on the darkened stage for ten minutes while he or she was looking out at the audience, no one ever took them up on their challenge.

A few years ago, the Royal hosted a show by Quebec entertainer André-Phillipe Gagnon. After the performance, Morris and Heemskerk joined Tex, the star's road manager, at the local pub. Tex was an older man who had many years' experience in the entertainment business. They had not been there long when Tex turned to his two companions and said, "You didn't tell me you had a guest in the theatre."

Heemskerk and Morris looked at each other, unsure what they had heard. Did he think they had brought a non-paying guest back stage to see the show? They finally asked him what he meant.

"I have one in my theatre too. If you don't talk to them they create nothing but trouble." Morris and Heemskerk realized that he meant a ghost. Although no one had mentioned the presence, Tex had sensed that the Royal Theatre was haunted.

In 1990, the World Wide Church of God, based in Pasadena, California, booked the Royal for a week-long engagement. The meetings were major events, with satellite dishes installed outside to broadcast the show over the church's television network. Since they had experience with the operation of these meetings, the church's own staff supervised many of the technical details. The job of clean-up, however, fell to the theatre's night custodian. About three a.m., he was vacuuming the carpet in the lobby when he happened to look up and see a man leaning over the balcony railing. Although the church people had been gone for over an hour, he assumed someone had fallen asleep in one of the upstairs rooms and had just woken up. He shut off the vacuum cleaner and went up the lobby stairs to investigate, but to his surprise he found no one. He noted nothing unusual: the bank of television monitors that the church had installed upstairs had been turned off because the network wasn't on the air.

He returned to the lobby somewhat concerned, but thought that the individual — a perfectly ordinary-looking man — had found his own way out. Several minutes later he looked up from his vacuum cleaner to see the man standing in the same spot. Leaving the machine running the custodian hurried upstairs once again to find nothing in the balcony. Upset, he returned to the lobby and shut off his vacuum cleaner. To his surprise he was suddenly aware of a hissing sound coming from the balcony. When he investigated, he found that every monitor installed upstairs had been turned on — the hissing sound was static coming from the speakers.

The custodian was so shaken that he immediately left the building and stood on the street corner in front of the theatre. While he didn't wish to return, he was also aware that the people from the World Wide Church of God would be arriving in the morning, and the building had not been cleaned. After two hours, during which he was torn between fear and duty, he steeled his resolve, went inside, turned on all the lights, and finished the job. After that, though, the service routine changed: the custodians at the Royal and McPherson theatres worked together, so that they were never alone in either building. Moreover, the cleaning of the Royal was done last, so that they worked there in the morning rather than at night. Later, the graveyard janitorial shift was dropped entirely in favour of daytime cleaning.

Even so the strange incidents did not end entirely. One day in the spring of 1996, the current custodian, Harvey Ratson, was cleaning the ladies' washroom downstairs. There were other people in the theatre at the time, and the last thing on his mind was the ghost. He was standing in the middle of the floor and had begun to turn around when suddenly he felt someone pat him on the head three times. He looked around, but no one was there. The three pats were distinctive — Ratson is convinced it wasn't his imagination. Nor could it have been a living person. "Nobody," he said, "goes pat, pat, pat on the top of your head to get your attention."

## THE SAGEBRUSH THEATRE

Regardless of the merits of the play, the difference between a good and a bad performance can be the result of nothing more than a missed cue or a "muffed" line. Given human nature, then, it is not surprising that such difficulties may be blamed on hands working mischievously behind the scenes. Such is the case at Kamloops' Sagebrush Theatre, where a ghost named Albert is said to reside. Although Albert's identity has never been positively established, tradition has it that he is the ghost of the first man to be executed in that city.

\* \* \* \* \*

According to David Ross, the Western Canada Theatre Company's managing director, most of Albert's tricks are rather juvenile. "It's basically things like somebody will hang a costume at a certain place backstage, and when they come back next day it's not there." Yet there is more to the happenings at the Sagebrush Theatre than the occasional missing article. For stage manager John Reilly, "It's generally the feeling that someone else is there." Even when there is not another person in the theatre, members of the Sagebrush staff often have the feeling of being observed.

Albert sometimes makes his presence known during performances. Once a technician observed a man dressed in old-fashioned clothes standing on one of the catwalks high above the stage. Because she was in a hurry she had no time to make a closer examination, but she called up to the control booth through her headset telling them to watch the intruder. While it was impossible for anyone to exit the catwalks without being seen by the men and women in the control booth, no one observed him leave. Nor did a later search of the building reveal anyone hiding there.

Former technical director Roger Lantz once reported that a stagehand had a similar experience. The man was up on the catwalk controlling the spotlight when he glanced to his side and saw a man sitting on the gantry. When he looked again the man had disappeared.

On another night, prior to a performance, two members of the crew separately saw a man sitting, each time, in the same theatre seat. Tempting fate, Lantz sat down in it and said, "Hey Albert, I'm sitting in your seat. What are you going to do about it?" That evening Lantz was controlling the sound board, and as he began, nothing seemed to go right. Audio levels were all wrong, sound that was supposed to come out of the speaker stage left came out of its opposite number, stage right, and audio cues were missed, with the result that it was the worst performance of his career. After that he never baited Albert again.

On one occasion, Lantz was working in the theatre when he heard a distinctive plink, plink, plink noise coming from the paint area back stage. It sounded like a number of small, hard objects falling one after the other onto the hard surface of the paint sink. When he investigated he found that the bottom of the sink was covered with small pebbles. He had no idea where the objects had come from, but he had certainly heard them fall. This was not an isolated incident — on several other occasions, tiny stones would be found at the bottom of the paint sink.

At times, Albert has taken a dislike to certain members of the crew. Once, during a rehearsal, a stagehand standing high in the fly gallery suddenly saw a bag of peanuts sail past him. There was no one standing in the direction from which the object came, nor was it likely that another crew member had thrown it — the fly gallery was no place for practical jokes.

The happenings at the Sagebrush Theatre have been seen not only by those connected with the stage — custodial staff have also witnessed unusual incidents. When Bill Graham, the head custodian at Kamloops Senior Secondary School, worked the night shift, he was always struck by the feeling that someone was watching him. Other custodial staff have had even stranger experiences. A few years ago a janitor reported that the removable boards which covered the orchestra pit had suddenly begun to vibrate and then roll like a wave. "Some [staff] have quit, some have taken off," Graham recalled. One afternoon he gave a tour of the theatre to a new janitor before she was to begin her first graveyard shift. When he mentioned the theatre was haunted, she told him that she didn't believe in ghosts. However, that night as she was vacuuming the lobby, the cord on her machine pulled away from the wall outlet. As she picked up the line to replug it, she noted that it was now tied in knots. Undoing the line, she once again plugged it in, only to have the vacuum cleaner stop a few minutes later. For a second time the cord had been pulled from the wall outlet, and as she picked it up she observed that once again it was tied in knots. This was too much for her — she didn't even finish her shift.

Albert, though, is apparently more than a simple prankster. On one occasion, the ghost intervened to prevent a serious accident. John Reilly related what happened to a technician who was in the theatre alone. She had gone up on one of the catwalks to practise using the spotlight. Suddenly she heard a voice calling up to her to put on her safety harness (a fall off the catwalk would have meant serious injury or death). Thinking that it must have been another crew member who had come in, and feeling somewhat guilty about her breach of safety rules, she put on the harness. Minutes later the spotlight suddenly broke away from its moorings, plunging to the floor 40 feet below. Had she not been wearing her harness, the woman would probably have been dragged off the catwalk with the falling object.

One important unanswered question is the identity of the ghost nicknamed Albert. Many theatre people believe he is actually Arnold Mallot (or Malot), the 23-year-old bartender from O'Keefe's Saloon at Eagle Pass near Revelstoke. Newspaper accounts of the time give a graphic description of the events that led to Mallot's untimely death. On August 9, 1885, a group of men was sitting at a table near the bar playing cards when a fight broke out. Mallot intervened, confiscating the deck of cards, which apparently angered one of the players, a man named Andrew Johnson, who reached behind the bar when Mallot's back was turned and grabbed a fistful of cigars. He then left the saloon, got on his horse and rode in the direction of his camp. When Mallot was told what Johnson had done, he grabbed his rifle, saddled up, and rode out after the thief. When he was a short distance from Johnson, Mallot opened fire, killing the man instantly.

Mallot was apprehended and taken to Kamloops for trial where he was found guilty of murder and sentenced to die by the rope. It would be another 14 months, though, before the penalty was exacted. On a cold November morning in 1886, Mallot faced his executioner.

The story of the death of the quick-tempered bartender might have been forgotten had it not been for the action of the

Kamloops council which, in 1939, decided that the bodies at the Lorne Street Cemetery should be moved to city property on Pleasant Street. Thus, the remains of many of Kamloops' pioneers were removed to plots opposite the high school. When rumours of strange happenings at the Sagebrush Theatre began to circulate, it was not surprising that some people connected the incidents with one of the Pleasant Street Cemetery's best-known residents.

While this theory is speculative at best, Mallot's story has a romantic quality that many people find appealing. Some Kamloops residents even contend that his punishment was too severe, for the man the bartender shot was a thief. Yet, for some members of the Sagebrush Theatre staff, questions concerning the ghost are academic. "I just accept the fact that he's here," Roger Lantz told a reporter during a 1989 interview. "There are times when you have that feeling you're not alone, but I don't think about it."

\* \* \* \* \*

*The Sagebrush Theatre in Kamloops, as seen from the Pleasant Street Cemetery.*
(PHOTO BY THE AUTHOR)

Albert Mallot may not be the only ghost who wandered away from the Pleasant Street Cemetery. A couple living near the grave-yard in the early 1970s had periodic visits from a spirit they called Herbie. "If we left the house and turned off all the lights," the man recalled, "[we'd] come back and there'd be a light on in the basement; there'd be a light on upstairs." The couple owned an inexpensive record player that had been set up in the living room. One difficulty with the machine was that it did not have a working power switch — to turn it off, one had to pull the plug out from the wall. Because of their concern regarding fire, the couple always unplugged the device before leaving the house, but when they returned it was not uncommon to find the power connected and a record playing.

Another of the ghost's favourite tricks was to alter the brightness control on the television so that the screen would become almost black. If, however, they told him to leave the television alone the image would return to normal. As often happens in the case of apparently harmless ghosts such as Herbie, the man and woman were sorry to lose him when they moved away.

## THE TOWNE THEATRE

According to local lore, Vernon's Towne Theatre is haunted by the ghost of a former projectionist, but neither the man's name nor why, after death, he has come back, is known. What can be said without question is that often the scariest happenings in the theatre have taken place off the screen.

\* \* \* \* \*

Although the lobby is bright and modern, many of the staff believe the Towne Theatre is haunted. Manager Matt Huebner is the first to admit that the building is the scene of many eerie happenings. A minor incident concerned a poster for an upcoming Jean Claude Van Damme motion picture that refused to stay in place. While other posters remained in the permanent, wall-mounted frame, this particular advertisement kept falling to the floor. The reason, Huebner concluded, may have been that the paper was cut slightly smaller, and therefore could be pulled free of the wall by gravity. "At the same time I find it kind of weird," he noted, "that it doesn't fall down during the day when I'm here or during the evening when we're working. But when I come in the next day it's down."

Other unexplained occurrences are common. When an acting manager went into the building to set up for the next showing he didn't bother to lock the front doors. When he prepared to leave, however, he was surprised to find the doors he had left unlocked were now secure. Since the main doors couldn't be locked without the keys, and at the time he was the only person in the city who had a set, he was at a loss to explain how it had happened.

Often the staff have heard a heavy tread on the stairs leading to the projection room. The sound of each step creaking is so distinctive it is impossible to mistake it for anything else. Yet Huebner has heard the noise when he has been alone in the building, working either downstairs in his office or up in the projection room. Huebner is not the only one to have been disturbed by footsteps: over the years many other staff have heard them. The janitors, who regularly begin work in the early hours of the

*The Towne Theatre in Vernon.* (COURTESY OF DIANE BELYK)

*The make-up platter in the Towne Theatre, where projectionists are often disturbed by phantom footsteps.* (COURTESY OF DIANE BELYK)

morning, have also reported hearing footsteps, followed by a jingling sound, as if someone was playing with a set of keys.

Sometimes footsteps are heard walking across the wooden floor of the projection room. Often when the staff are working at the large make-up platter — where the reels are prepared prior to loading on the projector — they will feel the floor sink as if someone had walked up and were standing directly behind them. Huebner recalled that at such times he could feel the hair on the nape of his neck bristle. A few years earlier, a projectionist was alone in the building, sitting on the floor attempting to repair something on the make-up platter, when he was aware that someone was standing behind him. As he moved to get up, he struck his head on the rim of the platter, with the result that the wound required four stitches to close.

The history of the building goes back many years. It was built as a dance hall some time after the turn of the century. In 1939, the original structure was completely renovated and reopened as part of the Famous Players chain. Then named the Capitol, it was one of the largest motion-picture theatres in the interior. Over the years, with changes in both technology and the public's taste, the theatre has been refurbished many times.

The last major renovation took place five years ago, when the building became part of the Towne Theatre organization. At that time a firm was hired to clean the 500 seats in the auditorium. One evening the crew had come in through the rear door of the building and left some of their equipment at one side of the stage while they returned to their truck to get more supplies. When they came back, all the equipment they had previously brought had been moved to the opposite end of the stage, a distance of about 30 feet. Later, as they worked, they were amazed to hear the auditorium suddenly fill with music: the theatre's public-address system had apparently turned itself on and begun running the tape of background music. After that, the cleaners were reluctant to be left in the building on their own.

\* \* \* \* \*

There are more haunted theatres in North America than most people would suppose. The Mount Baker Theatre in Bellingham, Washington, and the Liberty Theatre in Astoria, Oregon, are two of the more famous Northwest cinemas reputed to be haunted. In Alberta, the old Canmore Opera House, which was moved from Canmore to Calgary's Heritage Park in the 1960s, is said to contain the presence of a man sitting in the audience, and productions at the old Grand Theatre in London, Ontario, sometimes include the ghost of the former manager.

# CHAPTER FOUR

# Haunted Hotels and Pubs

L ike houses, hotels are places where people live and sometimes die. Thus, it is not surprising that so many of these places are frequented by ghosts. The following stories are about some of British Columbia's haunted inns.

## THE HAUNTED YEW

While no record exists of the brutal murder of a young Indian woman on South Pender Island many years ago, it may be a mistake to dismiss the story as mere folklore. According to many of the staff of the Bedwell Harbour Island Resort, the victim's ghost continues to make her presence known. Also, at the scene of the crime there remains a grim reminder of the heinous deed.

\* \* \* \* \*

As far as is known, the first large vessel to visit Bedwell Harbour was the Spanish schooner, *Horcasitasa,* which dropped anchor there in 1791. Since then the bay has had a reputation for being a safe and pleasant anchorage. The many springs in the area permitted ships to restock supplies of fresh water while the narrow entrance gave protection from the worst winter storms. Even before the arrival of the Europeans, though, the natives had considered one place, a rocky point jutting from the east side of Bedwell Harbour, to be taboo as a result of a great Indian battle that had taken place on that spot. While natives from Vancouver Island continue to come occasionally to collect shellfish, the 16-acre Indian reserve that adjoins the resort is usually uninhabited — uninhabited, that is, by the living. A number of tales are told about a tall warrior spirit who is seen walking through this land.

Yet the most active Bedwell ghost seems to have a more recent history. The presence is said to be that of a young native clam digger who was murdered while fleeing two European men who had rowed from a ship to the island. She ran along the shore, but couldn't outdistance them. They caught the woman by a small yew tree and, after raping her, one of the men took a pair of oarlocks and beat her to death. As if to mark the terrible deed, the murderer took the oarlocks and drove them into the tree trunk where they remain to this day. Now, however, the tree has

*The old oarlocks, almost completely overgrown by the yew tree.* (COURTESY OF DIANE BELYK)

68

grown around these gruesome locks so that only a small part of them is visible.

The first store on South Pender Island was built by F. X. Hodgson near the reserve in 1933. In the 1960s, a resort was completed at Bedwell Harbour, and over the years, the operation has been enlarged. Although the harbour offers excellent moorage for boats, the land above the bay is hilly. A pub, store, and small cafe were built on the flat land near the water while the cabins and restaurant extended up the hill. Although ghostly activity has been reported in other areas of the property, the pub, which was built beside the yew tree, seems to be the most active spot. One day several years ago, a man working on the plumbing under the building was surprised to feel a hand on his shoulder. When he turned around, no one was there. The frightened plumber made a quick exit and couldn't be persuaded to return.

In 1994, Ken Mohammed had a summer job working in the kitchen of the Bedwell Harbour Island Pub. One day as he was putting hamburger patties on the grill, the door to the large walk-in refrigerator opened suddenly. The door had a latch mechanism and considerable effort was needed to open it. Curious, he turned to face the refrigerator and as he did, the door swung shut again. It was possible to enter the refrigerator from the pub side, but that small door was intended only to allow access to the cases of beer from the front. Mohammed went into the pub and asked if anyone had entered the refrigerator from the wrong way, but no one admitted having done so.

During that same summer, two young, off-duty resort workers had their own experience on the hill above the resort. They were not entirely sober when the incident occurred, but both men were sure of what they had witnessed: a misty, glowing shape. While, the next day, each man had to endure the good-natured skepticism of their friends, neither would change his story. They had not said exactly where the incident had occurred, but Mohammed decided to investigate the general area and see what he could discover. He didn't notice anything unusual until he reached the area where several trash barrels were stored. Suddenly he was overcome by the feeling he wasn't alone. He was sure that someone or something unseen was there. When Mohammed approached the two workers, they confirmed the shape had materialized near the trash barrels. Mohammed later discovered that in the past, the ghost of a tall Indian warrior had been seen in the same general area.

When Dave Fontain was hired as bartender at the Bedwell pub in early 1996, he, his wife Karen, and their two children occupied one of the resort's large villas while they looked for a house of their own. They had been there less than a month when Karen decided to sleep in the children's room because both youngsters were sick. During the night, she was suddenly awoken by the measured slap, slap, slap, of bare feet upon a hard surface. As Karen lay awake, the footsteps stopped. Then she was aware of a woman's voice. "It wasn't really a yell, but it wasn't a moan either; it was just sort of 'ahhhh'," Karen reported later.

As she opened her eyes and looked toward the ceiling she was aware of a thick fog that seemed to pervade the room. Her first thought was that the villa was on fire and that the room had filled with smoke. As she climbed from her bed and stood up, though, she realised that there was no smell of burning. Standing outside her room, she could look into the kitchen and living room where the mist was thick. Karen, who is a firm believer in the paranormal, concluded that there wasn't a material cause for the phenomenon, and since there was nothing she could do she returned to bed. Only the next day, did she learn about the ghost of the murdered woman who was supposed to haunt the area.

The following night Karen was again sleeping in the children's room. As she was drifting off to sleep, she was suddenly aware that a cold hand was moving slowly up her right leg. There was no one in the room but Karen and the sleeping children. "Go away," Karen demanded, and the hand was suddenly withdrawn. Later that night she was awoken by her husband's voice saying, "You do realize this child is very sick, don't you?" She sat up and looked at her baby who was sleeping peacefully in her crib at the end of the bed.

Karen got up and looked into the living room, thinking that Dave was playing some sort of a joke on her, but he wasn't there. About this time, Dave was awoken from a deep sleep by someone's hand grabbing his shoulders and shaking him forcefully. The action was enough to bring him to full consciousness, but when he opened his eyes no one was there. Even as he lay there awake the shaking continued. For Dave, who wasn't inclined to believe in ghosts, the incident was unsettling.

Several months later, Karen and her friend Brandy Fitzpatrick had gone one afternoon to the latter's apartment, which was located on the hill almost directly above the haunted yew tree. The two women were sitting in the dining room and talking about some of the strange happenings at the resort when suddenly the outside door opened. They looked in the direction of the sound; there was no one to be seen. Karen got up and went outside but could find nothing to account for the occurrence. Brandy, who was so frightened that she didn't wish to remain alone in her apartment, quickly joined Karen outside.

The ghost who seems to inhabit the area around the old yew tree continues to make her presence known. Early in 1996, Karen and Dave Fontain bought some prints that they thought would brighten up the pub. One picture, however, would not remain on the wall. No matter how firmly Dave secured it, the print would come crashing to the floor. This also happened when no one had been on the premises; Dave sometimes opened the pub in the morning to discover that the piece of art had fallen down during the night. Karen noted that the scene closely resembled the spot behind the pub where the brutal murder was supposed to have taken place. She decided to take the print down and replace it with a picture from home: a framed poster advertising a Victoria sailboat race. As she expected, the new image seemed much more acceptable to the ghost. Unlike the print, the poster has never fallen from its place on the wall.

## SLIM AND HIS DOG

Although the ghost of an elderly man and his dog have frightened many of the people who have worked at Jake's Crossing Pub or its predecessor, the Port Moody Arms Pub on St. John's Street in Port Moody, the presence is entirely benign. It seems that Slim remains because he feels very much at home in the old building.

\* \* \* \* \*

When David James "Slim" Kirkpatrick became seriously ill in 1978 and was taken to Surrey Memorial Hospital, his long-time friend John Alvero often visited him. Slim had been acting as an unofficial caretaker at the Port Moody Arms Hotel, which was owned by John and his brother Meco. Slim and his dog, Jimmy Joe, a small black cocker spaniel, lived in the basement, in a earthen-floored room next to where the beer kegs were stored. The rude accommodation didn't seem to bother Slim, for although he was in his late 70s, he led an active life, and was seldom there long. Slim in his jeans and plaid shirt, accompanied by his dog, was a familiar sight on the streets of the city. Only after becoming sick did he spend much time in his room.

One day, after talking with Slim for a few minutes, John told his friend about his upcoming trip to Europe, and said he would see him when he returned. By the time John came home, though, Slim was dead. For John, the passing of the tall man with the iron-grey hair was particularly difficult, because he had known him a long time. John's feelings were shared by many of the staff and patrons of the

*Jake's Crossing, formerly known as the Port Moody Arms Hotel.* (PHOTO BY THE AUTHOR)

hotel. Patty Grotke, who began work there in 1973, recalled that he was the kind of man who would often wait until closing time to escort her to her car, "just to make sure everything would be all right."

The area where Slim had had his bed was dimly lit, so it was not surprising that many employees began to feel uncomfortable when they went down to the keg room. Grotke remembers that it was said half-jokingly around the bar that going to the basement might bring an unlucky person face-to-face with Slim's ghost. On occasion she had to go downstairs to change the lines of the soft-drink machines. "I was always frightened," she recalled, "because that's where Slim lived." At times she had the feeling that he was there watching her, yet she knew that she had nothing to fear from the man she had come to know so well. He would never have done anything to hurt her.

As long as the Alvero brothers operated the Port Moody Arms, unexplained incidents at the hotel were rare. However, in 1986, eight years after Slim's death, Meco and John sold the establishment to Mel and Jessie Schrader, a couple from Williams Lake. Though the Schraders did not make major changes, Slim's friends, the Alvero brothers, were no longer there. The character of the city was also changing. Once a small mill town, Port Moody had been swallowed by the growth of suburban Vancouver, and many of the regulars were no longer coming to the Arms.

One morning not long after taking over, Jessie Schrader had gone into the cocktail lounge to prepare the room for opening later that day. As she looked up she saw a plaid shirt behind the bar. Believing that an intruder had entered the premises she ran out of the room. When she returned to the lounge with other staff, moments later, no one was there.

Some time afterward, Theresa, Mel and Jessie's daughter, was working in the hotel. "In the office off the lounge," she recalled later, "there was an antique record player that never worked." While closing up one evening, she heard music coming from the office. When she went to investigate, Theresa was surprised to discover that the gramophone had begun to play. She watched the ancient needle move across the vinyl disk that was now on the turntable. Theresa called Terry Mattice, the custodian, but he was unable to discover a reason for the incident. No one admitted putting on a record or turning on the turntable.

On another evening, Theresa heard a commotion down in the basement where Slim's room had once been. She asked Terry to go down and investigate, and he found nothing. Jessie Schrader also had an experience in that part of the basement. She had gone downstairs to get something when suddenly the bulb that hung overhead went out. The area was now in total darkness. Jessie began to panic, for she had no idea how to find her way out. "Slim," Jessie said under her breath, "if you've ever been around I need you now." Immediately the light went on again. Jessie quickly made her way to the door. As she crossed the threshold, she said, "Thank you God, thank you Slim." Again, the basement light went out.

The first week Debbie Yurkoski began work as a waitress, she was sent downstairs to pick up supplies after the pub closed. When she entered the basement she was surprised to see a man leaning against the wall holding what she thought was a black coat. She immediately turned and ran upstairs where she found Terry

*A presence caught on film? This photo was taken in the basement of Jake's Crossing. The strange light in the foreground was not visible to photographer Wesley Frank when he took the picture.* (COURTESY OF WESLEY FRANK)

Mattice and told him what she had seen. Since she had recently started at the hotel she didn't know the story of Slim and the black cocker spaniel, Jimmy Joe. Terry told her not to be frightened, and that the old man in the basement wouldn't harm anyone.

The basement area was a favourite spot among waitresses wishing to do their shift tallies, because it was quiet and they were not likely to be disturbed. However, it was not uncommon for some staff to complain that they felt as if they were being watched. When other staff went downstairs to investigate, there was no sign of an intruder. One waitress refused to go downstairs to tally her receipts, but sat on the steps instead.

When bartender Maryann Rogodzinski worked the late shift, she had the responsibility of making sure that all the doors were secure after she left. When her husband Len arrived to pick her up, Maryann would have him double check to make sure everything was locked. One night Maryann and Len completed their usual routine. As they left, Len gave the main doors one final shake to make sure that they were securely bolted. When the manager arrived the next morning, the doors were unlocked. For Maryann and Len, there was no logical explanation, unless someone had a duplicate key. However, nothing was taken. "Sometimes," Maryann said, "I've been the butt end of his jokes." She has noted that the door to the refrigerator which has been latched shut will suddenly be standing open. Other bartenders have reported liquor bottles flying off shelves.

The Port Moody Arms was sold to John Kettlewell in 1988 and renamed Jake's Crossing, after J. T. (Jake) Scott, a city pioneer. The change in management seems to have been no deterrent to the ghost's activities. Waitress Nicole Henzel has frequently glimpsed Slim out of the corner of her eye as she has gone downstairs. In the pub, he continues to make his presence known. In the spring of 1996, Henzel had gone behind the bar to put a load of glasses into the automatic dishwasher. To her surprise one of the glasses suddenly rose about two feet in the air and landed in the trash.

In early April 1997, Blair Gelhorn, a relief cook, went downstairs to use the washing machine. He had no sooner filled the agitator basket with soiled linen than the machine suddenly turned on by itself. While the incident may have been the result of an electrical fault, there would seem to be no rational explanation for another occurrence a few days later. Gelhorn had gone to the basement with a load of laundry when he suddenly felt that he wasn't alone. As he turned his head to see if someone had come downstairs, he was surprised to see a chair five or six feet away from where he stood slowly move on its own. At first the young man couldn't believe his eyes — he was convinced that one of the other staff members was playing an elaborate practical joke. However, as he watched, the chair continued on a path that brought it steadily toward him. After a few minutes of its slow progress, it bumped against his knees. At that moment Gelhorn heard a whispered voice say, "Sit down." Declining the invitation, the young man ran upstairs to tell his fellow workers what had happened.

Not all the activity happened in the lounge and basement. Manager Elaine Grossman was going down the outside stairs at the back of the building when she saw a cat sitting there. By the time she looked again, though, it had disappeared. On another occasion, she was standing near the electrical room by the basement entrance when the door suddenly opened. She quickly left and returned with several other staff who searched the area, but they could find nothing. When Terry Mattice worked there in the late 1980s, and made rounds through the hotel hallway upstairs, he frequently heard footsteps behind him. When he turned around there was never anyone to be seen.

According to Al and Nellie Sholund, Slim may not be the only ghost who haunts the old hotel. Even many years before the elderly man's death, the building was the scene of many strange happenings. In the spring of 1956, the Sholunds lived at the Port Moody Arms for three months. The couple recalled that during the evening it wasn't unusual to hear the sound of feet passing along the hall. When they opened their door, the corridor would be empty.

Instead of a sprinkler system, mounted on the ceiling of the Sholunds' room was a large metal ball filled with flame retardant. The couple often saw this object begin to vibrate rapidly. At first they thought the movement may have been related to a train passing along the tracks nearby, but this clearly wasn't the case, for the ball would begin to shake even when no train was near.

At one time, the basement was used as a meeting room for various local organizations. Al Sholund recalled that it was not uncommon to prepare the room for an upcoming meeting and then lock it up at night, only to discover the next day that the chairs and tables had been moved around. "There are things in this place I just can't explain," he noted.

* * * * *

As far as Maryann Rogodzinski is concerned, Slim is a harmless presence who seems to enjoy the company of the staff and patrons of the establishment that had once been his home. She recalled a series of events several years ago, during the time she was working as a waitress. When she went downstairs to add up her accounts she would joke to the other staff that she was going to have a drink with Slim. This practice went on for some time until she took on the job of bartender. After that, her new responsibilities rarely involved visiting the basement. After a few days she noticed that everything seemed to being going wrong — items went missing, and glass breakage took an alarming upturn. She then decided that it would be wise to take a few minutes each day and visit Slim in the basement. Immediately she noted that the losses and breakages decreased.

## THE FACE AT THE WINDOW

Long ago, the Senator Hotel at 1212 Granville Street had been a respectable establishment, but during the Depression it fell on hard times and never recovered. Even during the 1940s and '50s when Granville Street, between Smithe and Hastings, was the heart of the city, the Senator was built several blocks too far south to benefit from the good times. Like other small hotels in the area, it catered to a down-and-out clientele living at the edge of the economic boom.

In the late 1960s Granville Street became the destination of many troubled teenagers from across Canada who saw Vancouver as the San Francisco of the North. Both the police and the city's social-welfare services were concerned as hundreds of young people made Granville Street's once-prosperous theatre district their home. Yet neither department ever found a successful answer to this problem. One solution the city attempted in 1980 was to turn the old Senator Hotel into a group residence for minors living on the street. Young people could thus be sure of a safe place to stay, and access to medical and social services. In 1983, the ancient hotel became home to a teenager, Ramona Harper, (not her real name) who was pregnant and alone.

From the beginning of her stay, Ramona noted that the staff seemed to be forever losing things. Keys, which were supposed to be in their possession all the time, would go missing, with the result that many of the residents were unjustly accused of playing pranks. The missing items usually turned up later in a place that had been previously searched.

Ramona had not been living at the Senator long when she became aware that the upstairs hall did not feel right. When she walked down it at night, she had an eerie sensation that someone was following her. Whenever she turned around, no one was there, but Ramona couldn't shake the feeling that she was being watched. Whatever it was, she was sure the "thing" was malevolent and wished her harm. It became her practice when she left her room, to run down the hall as fast as she could.

The bathroom on her floor also turned out to be a strange place. One day, Ramona went there to have a shower. The room was small, with a sink and toilet in the anteroom, and a shower stall with a glass door set into one wall. After she had turned off the water and was drying herself, she happened to glance below the glass shower door. To her surprise she could see a pair of bare legs standing there, as if someone was waiting to use the stall. What was visible was the lower third of the body of a young woman. The legs were olive-complexioned and the skin very smooth. Ramona vividly recalled locking the outside door — no one should have had access to the bathroom while she was using it. When she opened the door to the cubicle, the room was empty. By now Ramona felt frightened, for it should have been equally impossible for the young person to leave without being seen. As she grabbed the door knob, it kept spinning in her hand. Her screams summoned a child-care worker from the downstairs office, and he was able to use a key to open the door from the outside. After freeing Ramona he checked the inside handle. To her amazement, it worked perfectly.

On another occasion, Ramona had gone to bed and had almost fallen asleep when she was suddenly awakened by what sounded like a baby crying in the street below. She went to her window, which overlooked an ancient house next door that was rented by a group of punk rockers. To her surprise, the street lights revealed about 20 cats gathered in the yard and looking up at her room. While their behaviour was unusual, Ramona dismissed the incident and returned to bed. She had not yet fallen asleep when she heard what sounded like the high-pitched cry of a baby coming from directly outside her room. She got up again, went to the window and opened the curtain to see a cat sitting outside her window. While this may have explained the cry, there was no ledge outside her room: the cat had to have been perched in mid-air. "Out to here pregnant, I flew over my bed, fell over a chair, and went screaming down the stairs and told the child-care worker who was on duty about what I saw," Ramona recalled. When he went upstairs to investigate, however, the cat was gone.

Another frightening incident happened down the hall from where Ramona slept, in an area used by those living on that floor as a common room. One night, as Ramona was sitting watching television with Holly, another resident of the Senator, the young woman, for no apparent reason, suddenly got up and ran from the room. Surprised, Ramona looked around. To her amazement, she saw a man's face in the window. The person was old, with a long, narrow face partially hidden by a white beard. Frightened, Ramona also got up and ran downstairs. When she reached the office, Holly was already giving her description of the face she had seen to Mr. Funk, the child-care worker. It was almost identical to the person Ramona had seen.

When the child-care worker went upstairs with the two young women, the face had disappeared. Again, there was no ledge or fire escape where an intruder could have stood. Funk wondered if it had been an optical illusion produced by a reflection in the window, but the effect couldn't be repeated. After that incident, whenever she was in the common room, Ramona found herself glancing nervously toward the window, wondering if the old man would return.

One Saturday evening some time later, Ramona was in another resident's room trying on a pair of jeans with a waist wide enough to accommodate her growing abdomen. She happen to glance out the window which overlooked a narrow courtyard between the building's two wings. In one of the rooms a woman was apparently cleaning, for the bed was pushed so far up against the open window that a corner of the mattress extended beyond the sill. Ramona knew that the back section of the hotel was supposed to be unused. The rooms there had been stripped of their furnishings and the area sealed off. Moreover, the person working there was not Anna, their usual cleaning woman: she was a complete stranger.

Given the reputation of the building, both young women were convinced that what they were seeing was not a natural occurrence. They rushed downstairs to tell the staff on duty, but when they returned the window in the room opposite was closed and there was no sign of the cleaning woman. When the child-care worker went to investigate he found that the door to the back half of the hotel was locked and he had no key to get in.

Many of the workers at the group home remained skeptical of these stories since the happenings usually took place upstairs where the residents lived, and therefore were not witnessed by the staff. One day, though, Ramona was in the kitchen preparing something to eat. She had turned on the oven and placed a frozen dinner inside. When she went to retrieve it sometime later, she brushed against the door, and felt a searing pain in her leg where it contacted the hot surface. She quickly found a staff member to dress the wound, which had removed the surface layer of skin. When one of the workers went to examine the accident scene, he was surprised to note that the area of the stove that had touched Ramona was quite cool. This didn't make sense because Ramona's leg was clearly burnt. What was even more amazing was that when the bandage was taken off the next day, there was no sign of injury. It was as though it had healed overnight.

Before having her baby, Ramona was placed in a foster home. The following year the Senator closed as a group residence, apparently the result of an end to government funding. A short time later, the building reopened as the Ambassador Hotel. According to hotel staff, no paranormal incidents have been reported there recently.

It would be easy to jump to the conclusion that the youth residence was not haunted at all, but instead was invaded by a poltergeist. Indeed, unhappy teenagers are often the focus of the poltergeist's unwanted attention, and the young people living at the Senator had every reason to be dissatisfied with their lot in life.

*The Ambassador Hotel in Vancouver, formerly the Senator Hotel.* (COURTESY OF DIANE BELYK)

Yet the activity at the old hotel did not mirror typical poltergeist behaviour. These "ghosts" (there is some controversy about whether they are ghosts at all) are noisy and destructive, which was not the case at the youth residence. Although sightings are sometimes reported as part of poltergeist activity, apparitions are relatively rare. So what was really happening at the Senator? Like everything associated with the paranormal, the events at the old Granville Street hotel defy simple explanation.

## FRIDAY

Sometimes ghosts are quiet inhabitants, and this certainly seems to be the case with Friday, the presence some believe haunts the basement of the Princeton Hotel. Friday is a quiet resident — he is rarely heard and never seen, and there is nothing frightening about him. Those who visit the basement of the old hotel, however, often know he is there.

\* \* \* \* \*

81

Most of the details concerning Friday's early life are unknown, but what is clear is that he arrived as a Chinese immigrant to the province around the turn of the century. Many new arrivals were attracted to the mining activity in the area around Princeton, a town at the junction of the Tulameen and Similkameen rivers. As the years passed, it is likely that Friday accepted the job as handyman at the Princeton Hotel when he was no longer able to do the heavy physical labour demanded by the mining industry. The hotel had been built in 1910 by two area businessmen, Stan Garrison and William Broomfield. At the time it was one of the most modern in British Columbia, with hot and cold running water in every room and a barber shop in the lobby.

Friday's responsibilities included meeting the train at the station. He would sit at the depot patiently waiting for the sound of the engine as it pulled in and then he'd go and load the luggage of passengers destined for the hotel into the ancient Dodge panel truck. During the cold winter months, his last job before going to bed was to stoke the big coal furnace in the basement. He lived not far from the hotel's source of heat: he had converted an unused coal bin in the basement into his living quarters. Although the basement was dark and dusty, he lived quietly and never seemed to complain.

It would be wrong to suppose that Friday was simply an employee. He was a close friend of Broomfield's, the co-owner of the hotel, and the two frequently went hunting in the mountains around the town. On one such trip, Friday fell off the edge of a bluff, and Broomfield regarded it as a miracle that his friend survived with only minor injuries. Yet, for Friday, his escape from death turned out to be a relatively short reprieve. One day a few years later, while he was going to the basement, a stair tread splintered and broke under his weight, sending him tumbling head-over-heels down the steps. When he reached the bottom his head smashed into the corner of a wooden support pillar, splitting his skull open and killing him instantly. (It is still possible to see the man's blood and hair marking that pillar.)

According to current co-owner Carol Brodie, who has operated the hotel for 16 years, what is surprising about the dark, damp place where Friday died is its atmosphere: "It looks like it should be quite scary but it isn't — all this sinister darkness and everything." Yet she has no hesitation in going downstairs by herself. "For some reason I always credit it to Friday's presence down there."

The same feeling does not exist on the hotel's main floor. Although the pub is usually a cheery place when it's full of customers, if Brodie is alone there with the main lights off, the room becomes quite frightening. She has no sense of a protective spirit in that room.

The reason Friday does not make himself more known, Brodie believes, is the result of the quiet kindness he apparently demonstrated throughout his life. "When it comes right down to it," she says, "he really wouldn't want to frighten anybody."

## SUSIE WOO

Like Friday, Susie Woo was a Chinese worker employed in a mining-town hotel. Many of the details of her life have also been lost to history. She had apparently worked at the Zeballos Hotel for many years, but her background, the date she died, and the cause of her death are not clear. What is certain, though, is that some people believe Susie continues to walk the corridors of the building that was her home.

* * * * *

Hostelries, like houses, do not have to be old to be haunted, and this certainly is the case with the Zeballos Hotel. Built in 1939, during a gold rush on the west coast of Vancouver Island, the hotel had the flavour of the frontier. The first owner, H. H. Vickers, didn't wait for his first guests to come to him; he personally took reservations from his fellow passengers aboard the CPR steamer, *Princess Maquinna*, during its sailing to Zeballos. The boom didn't last long, however. The shortage of labour during the Second World War closed some mines. After the war the artificially low price for gold — it was pegged at $35 an ounce — made further mining uneconomical. Although the town was to make a partial recovery with the growth of the forest industry and renewed interest in mining in the early 1970s, Zeballos never lived up to the hopes of its first residents.

One of the early arrivals in the town was Susie Woo, who took on the job of laundress for the new hotel. During her years in Zeballos, Susie occupied Room 1, upstairs. Sometime in the late 1940s, Susie died there, apparently of natural causes.

After Susie's death, her old room was refurbished and rented out to guests, but it was not long before the former employee made her displeasure plain. Susie clearly didn't want anyone using the area she considered her own. On one occasion two guests came downstairs, claiming to have seen a ghost in their room, but the staff found nothing when they went to investigate. At another time, Susie reportedly chased three fishermen staying in her room down the stairs and into the lobby. The men were so frightened that they refused to return even to pick up their belongings.

Several staff members also reported strange happenings in the hotel. Pablo, the one-time handyman, saw her frequently until he forced himself to confront her. He told the apparition to go away and not come back, with the result that she never again appeared to him. Employees didn't have to see Susie to know she was around. Sharon Brown, who was a waitress in the hotel's restaurant in 1986, noted, "Any time anything odd happens — doors opening and shutting — people just say 'There goes Susie again'."

In 1996, manager Mark Whyte had not been at the hotel long before he too was aware of odd happenings. When he arrived, he used Room 1 for his sleeping quarters. At first he didn't notice anything unusual, but gradually he began to feel uncomfortable. He would awaken during the night with the feeling that someone was in the room with him. On other occasions, he would hear footsteps going down the hall, but when he'd open the door to look, no one would be there.

Like many ghosts, Susie seems to make her presence known. One day Whyte had gone from the laundry room upstairs to a room he used as storage space. After looking through some of his belongings, he turned out the light and then shut and locked the door. "When I came out," he said later, "I made sure it was shut because I had a lot of personal things in there." At the end of the hall, though, he glanced back to see that the door was open. He returned to the laundry room after closing and locking the door again. When he finished his task he went upstairs only to discover the door to the storage room standing open again. The light, which he clearly remembered turning out, was now on. None of his belongings had been disturbed, but Whyte found the incident unsettling.

Although Whyte no longer lives in Room 1, he continues to use the space as an office. To date, Susie has not objected to this arrangement.

## THE HAUNTED FOUR MILE HOUSE

Many researchers have noted that paranormal activity usually increases during periods of building reconstruction, when walls are ripped out, ceilings replastered, and flooring removed. When Graham and Wendy Haymes bought a condemned roadhouse a few miles north of Victoria in 1979, they planned to turn it into a store selling antique reproduction furniture. The couple also intended to include a tea room on the premises. However, as renovations began, the owners of what is now Four Mile House began to experience many strange happenings.

\* \* \* \* \*

Four Mile Hill House was built by Peter Calvert in the 1850s as a stopping place for stage coaches on the Metchosin road. It was said that to make sure they stopped, the owner had a parrot who sat in the front window. Every time a coach passed by, the bird was trained to scream, "Whoa," thereby bringing the horses to a stop. Thinking that the animals were demanding a rest, the drivers had their passengers partake of the inn's hospitality. Whether the tale was true or not is unknown, but there is little doubt the business had an interesting and colourful history.

As the automobile replaced the horse, and frequent stops were no longer necessary, the establishment fell on hard times. The low point in the roadhouse's existence came after the Second World War when the place was bought by an former serviceman who called it the Lantern Inn. Nicknamed the "Green Latrine," the facility catered to sailors on leave from the nearby navy base. As an unlicensed nightclub, where a bottle of scotch, rye or gin was kept under the table, the place became a favourite among local prostitutes who entertained their clients in the upstairs rooms. During one of the recent renovations Wendy Haymes discovered several items of silk lingerie that had been hidden in the attic.

When Graham and Wendy inspected the dilapidated building, they were already aware that the building was supposed to be haunted. These tales didn't dissuade them from making the purchase, for whatever ghosts might be present, Wendy felt, were probably friendly. As it turned out, she was right.

The couple began making extensive renovations. The task wasn't easy, for they couldn't afford outside contractors, and Graham's job took him away for long periods. Wendy became pregnant not long after beginning the project, and since she had several other small children to care for, she found it difficult to help her husband.

One day, as Graham was leaving for work, he asked his wife to take the industrial vacuum cleaner they had rented upstairs and vacuum up the mounds of drywall dust that had collected there. By this time she was almost ready to give birth, and her back was giving her a lot of pain. Worse, the machine they had rented did not work well. After a few minutes she stood up, rubbed her back and said to the spirits, "All right you guys, make this worth my while because I'm getting pretty tired of this." As she bent down to continue her work she noticed an American five-cent piece dated 1867 on the spot where she had just vacuumed. Wendy took that to be a sign that all their hard work would be rewarded.

Often after Wendy and her husband stopped work in the early hours of the morning, they would go to bed only to hear noises coming from upstairs. To Wendy, it sounded like hammering and sawing, as if the household ghosts were continuing work where the couple had left off.

According to Wendy, the ghosts had definite opinions on how the renovations should take place. One day her younger sister Leslie was upstairs helping with the work while Wendy was in the kitchen. Suddenly she heard her sister scream. From where she was, Wendy could hear Leslie running down the steps with what sounded like another set of footsteps in close pursuit. The young woman burst into the kitchen exclaiming, "This guy touched me from behind and then chased me down the stairs." Wendy searched the house but there was no one to be seen. The ghost, Wendy believes, was simply trying to get Leslie's attention, to show her how to do the work properly.

Later, Graham and Wendy took a house across the street from the building that by now had been turned into a tea room and store. One winter day about 1984, before they had opened for afternoon tea, the waitress approached Wendy who was in the kitchen and said, "Where did that guy come from?"

"What guy?" Wendy asked.

"There was a guy sitting in the tea room and I don't know how he got there."

Wendy asked what the man looked like, and the waitress described someone slightly balding with dark hair. He was wearing a dark trench coat, unbuttoned, over a 1940s-style suit. On the table was an open briefcase from which he had evidently removed some papers that he was studying.

"Well," Wendy said, "he's been there for the whole week and he's been driving me crazy." Although she was able to see him out of the corner of her eye, she noted, "Every time I'd spin around, he'd be gone, but the chair would be slightly ajar so I knew he'd been there."

After a few minutes, Wendy went across the street to her house where her mother was baby-sitting. When she told the older woman about the incidents, her mother admitted that the previous day, when she had gone to place flowers on the tables in the tea room, she had seen a man sitting there. Her description of him tallied with what her daughter and the waitress had seen. At the time the building was again undergoing renovations, and Wendy feels that this was the reason for the ghost's appearance.

By 1988, the furniture store was closed and a pub and a restaurant opened in its place. The dining room, particularly, is the centre of many strange happenings. In the morning before the first patrons are shown to their seats, the staff often report hearing a clinking sound, as if a teaspoon is being struck against the side of a cup. Staff also report the sound of footsteps walking upstairs, while Wendy has heard children crying at times when no youngsters have been on the premises.

Probably the most ancient ghost to haunt the site is that of Jake Matteson who, sometime after 1850, was the first European to own the land. Matteson, it was said, kept his savings in gold down a well on his property. He intended to use the money to build a home there before sending for his sweetheart in Scotland, but died suddenly before he could begin his project. The gold was never discovered, and there are some who believe that Jake is still watching over his money.

A later ghost believed to haunt Four Mile House is that of Margaret Gouge who lived at the roadhouse during the second half of the 19th century. She was known for her love of flowers, and has been seen looking down from what is now the laundry room into the well-maintained garden. She is wearing a full length gown and appears entranced by what she sees.

Although she doesn't haunt the premises itself, another ghost has been seen not far away. She is known as the Lady in White. When her sea-captain husband sailed away she apparently came to stay with the Calvert family who were relatives. She would spend many hours walking the rugged shore near the inn as she waited for her husband's return. Sadly, she became ill and died before his ship came home, and her ghost has been seen near Thetis Point standing upon the rocks and looking vainly out to sea. In the Four Mile pub there is a beautiful stained-glass image of the Lady in White. It is a poignant reminder of a time when ships sailed from Victoria into the vast, silent waters of the North Pacific never to be seen or heard from again.

*The Four Mile House, near Victoria.* (PHOTO BY THE AUTHOR)

# CHAPTER FIVE

# Haunted Highways

For many people, the ghosts that may linger along the streets and highways of this province seem particularly frightening. These spectres are, after all, difficult to avoid, for they are very public spirits. Drive around the bend of any road, and indeed you may come face-to-face with one of them.

## THE PHANTOM OF HIGHWAY 1

In the spring of 1975, John and Janice Bradley left Vancouver to visit John's brother, Dave, and his wife, Judy, who were living in Kamloops. The decision to go had been made at the last minute, and it was not until after dinner that they finally loaded their suitcases into the trunk of their automobile and got under way. For the young couple, the trip was particularly exciting for neither John nor Janice had ever been to Kamloops. Although there was a chill in the air, it was a beautiful night for a romantic moonlit drive. They reached Hope a little before midnight, and took the north fork along Highway 1 that follows the eastern edge of the Fraser Canyon. They had planned to stop for the night at the small town of Spences Bridge, beyond the end of the canyon, but in the few motels scattered along the highway, all the lights were out. John and Janice had little choice but to push on to the junction town of Cache Creek where they were sure a motel room would be available.

By now it was after one a.m., and there was almost no traffic on the road. Even the drivers of the big transport trucks had pulled over to get a few hours of sleep. The couple had been on the road more than three hours, but they were not particularly tired — the view of the glittering night sky in this part of British Columbia kept them awake.

John was behind the wheel as they approached the brow of a small hill about half way between Spences Bridge and the turn-off to Ashcroft. Along one side of the road Janice noticed an number of shacks, obviously abandoned. No lights were visible in the windows, the walls leaned crazily in one direction or the other and on most, the roofs seemed to be falling in. Suddenly their high beams illuminated the back of a woman walking along the edge of the highway. As they drew closer, John and Janice could see she was short, with black hair cut bluntly above her shoulders. Janice estimated that she was less than five feet tall, which, combined with her straight, black hair, made it seem likely that she was of Asian descent. Her clothes, though, did not look like anything John or Janice had seen before. She wore short, dark pants that came down only as far as her calf, and a dark vest over a puffy-sleeved white blouse. On her feet, she had flat, black leather shoes.

Even though it was a beautiful night, it seemed strange to Janice that the woman was out in this lonely spot without a coat. The way she was walking was also unusual. She was moving quickly, taking short, mincing steps, with her elbows bent, and arms swinging rapidly back and forth. Janice's first thought was that the woman had had car trouble and was forced to walk for help, but she hadn't noticed any vehicles parked at the side of the highway. Another possibility, Janice reasoned, was that her car had slid off the road and was now out of sight. "Pull over closer to the shoulder, John," Janice said, "and I'll see if she needs help."

As John drew up beside the walker, Janice rolled down her window. "Excuse me, madam," she began, "do you need..." The woman jerked her head in their direction. The movement of the head was strange, as though the motion was not altogether human. The face, which was as white as porcelain, lacked eyebrows, but was defined by a mouth twisted into a vicious snarl, and eyes so electrifying that Janice was later unable to find words to describe their appearance. The pupils were incredibly large and darker than anything she had ever seen. Both John and Janice were sure that whatever it was they were looking at was not human.

John uttered an oath, pushed his foot down on the gas pedal, and the automobile sped away. Janice quickly turned around to look out the rear window, but no one was there. The woman seemed to have vanished. John did not slow down until he could see the lights of Ashcroft in the distance. "What the hell was that?" he finally said. Janice had no idea.

The following day, Janice phoned the Ashcroft detachment of the RCMP to enquire if there had been an accident along that section of the highway. Nothing had been reported to the police. Still unsettled, she asked the clerk whether there were any Oriental families living in the area. No, came the reply, not for some time. Once, though, the woman said, there had been a number of Chinese people living on a few farms, but the old dwellings had long been abandoned and were falling down. They could be still seen beside the highway.

* * * * *

Janice's description of the walker's apparel is certainly consistent with what a Chinese woman might have worn almost one hundred years ago. An examination of the newspapers around the turn of the century reveals that Ashcroft indeed had a small but active Chinese population. "A marriage in Chinatown was an event a day or two ago," stated the *Ashcroft Journal* on December 22, 1900. "The groom is known in business as You Lee. ... The bride's name could not be learned. She has been a resident of the coast for some time." Could this person, or another woman in a similar circumstance, be the ghost who haunts Highway 1? While it is possible, there is little likelihood of ever knowing for sure.

## THE LADY IN BLACK

The rural settlement of Sooke and its outlying areas west of Victoria have more than their share of road phantoms. The story of the hitchhiking ghost of China Flats was included in *Ghosts*, but another phantom of the local roads also deserves mention. An often-repeated tale in the Sooke area concerns a spectre locals believe may be the ghost of Louisa May Stiff, a one-time school teacher from the district. She can be seen, dressed in black, with a singularly forlorn expression, standing at the side of East Sooke Road. While such stories are the stuff of legend, the tale of the Lady in Black may be more than a myth.

\* \* \* \* \*

In October, 1989, office administrator Evelyn Beaulac was on her way to work early one morning when she saw what she thought was a ghost. As she was driving along Gillespie Road near its inter-section with East Sooke Road, she spotted the figure of a woman standing alone. As she recalled:

I was coming around the corner. It was foggy but not enough so you couldn't see the road. I saw her. She scared me. She had such a white, white face. She had [on] dark clothing. It was raining and cold and this lady was very wet, but she didn't move.

As time passed, Beaulac was less sure that what she had seen was an apparition, but the woman, who behaved so peculiarly in the rain, fit perfectly the description of the Lady in Black.

For Michel and Marion Desroches, there was little doubt that what they encountered less than a month later was a ghost. It was late one night in early November, when Michel and his wife were driving along East Sooke Road. As they rounded a curve, Marion recalled, "Suddenly we came across this figure at the yellow line on the left side [of the road]."

They described the woman as wearing a black, Edwardian-style dress, a wide-brimmed hat, and button shoes. Like Evelyn

Beaulac, Michel and Marion were surprised that the woman was standing motionless in the pouring rain. "She had a very pale, grey face. She was not looking at us. It was like she was looking through us."

Unlike the Beaulac incident when the figure had been soaked by the rain, Marion noted that despite the weather, the woman's clothing was dry. Although she looked solid, the couple had little doubt that the apparition had no physical contact with this world.

An interesting question concerns the identity of the Lady in Black. For many years she was assumed to be the ghost of Louisa May Stiff, a local school teacher who was thrown from a buggy on East Sooke Road. The difficulty with this explanation is that the woman did not die because of the accident, but lived on for a number of years. She in fact died in Victoria in the 1920s as a result of cancer. At least as far as anyone knows, there is nothing to draw the ghost of Miss Stiff to that lonely stretch of island road. If not Louisa May Stiff, then who haunts East Sooke Road?

There have been no recent reports of appearances by the Lady in Black, but this does not mean she has been absent from her usual haunts. Frequently such tales do not make it to the local press, and thus written records of her visits are not preserved. Given her ghostly history, it would be surprising if on rainy autumn days, she no longer stands beside East Sooke Road with that sad look upon her pale face.

\* \* \* \* \*

In 1986, East Sooke Road was the location of another sighting. On this occasion, though, the apparition was not the Lady in Black. About noon one day, Calvin Reichelt was driving along a stretch of the road near the ocean; the weather was wet and the visibility reduced by a fine mist. Still, Reichelt had no doubt about what he saw: a good-looking young woman about 25 years old wearing a long white dress. "There she was," he reported later. "I stopped, like a fool, to give her a ride and she just walked through the car and into the mist." Like the Lady in Black, the identity of this ghost is unknown.

## DANCING MARY

The old Comox Hill Road is the haunt of Dancing Mary, one of this route's more interesting ghostly legends. As is often the case with folk tales, many of the facts have been lost, but the elements that make the story memorable remain.

More than a century ago, an attractive young Kwakiutl woman named Mary fell in with a white man who lived near the town of Comox. According to those who knew him, when sober the man was pleasant enough, but when he was the worse for liquor he became a monster. During these drunken rages, it was said, he would brutally beat the unfortunate woman. One day Mary disappeared and was never seen again. While everyone in town believed that she had been murdered by her violent husband, no proof was ever found — he simply claimed she had left him. The man eventually moved away from the shack he and Mary had occupied on Comox Hill and, as time passed, the story was all but forgotten.

Mary, though, became the topic of conversation again when one night a farmer arrived in town with an unusual story. He said he was about half way up Comox Hill when his horse suddenly reared. In the middle of the road was the figure of a young Indian woman dancing alone. He had no doubt that what he was observing was something unearthly: the shape before him was surrounded by an envelope of blue light.

When no further sightings were reported, the incident was almost forgotten until, during the Second World War, a young airman happened to be riding his bike back to the base at Comox. The hour was late, when the man reached the mid-point of the hill. To his surprise he was suddenly aware of a luminous blue mist on the road in front of him. Held within the fog was the figure of a young woman with arms extended, dancing gracefully. As he watched she appeared to beckon him closer. The airman was terrified, but the way to his base was ahead, and he was more frightened about what his sergeant would do if he overstayed his pass. Head lowered, he pedalled quickly through the blue mist that blocked his way. As he reached the edge of it he suddenly shivered — it was as though the night had become abruptly colder — but seconds later he emerged into the warmth of the late spring evening.

While the young man was not familiar with the story of Mary, many of the older Comox residents recalled the incident that happened on the same road half a century earlier. They wondered if this was indeed the ghost of the murdered woman, returned once again.

\* \* \* \* \*

During the Second World War, Comox Hill was the site of many unexplained occurrences. At least four people reported seeing a ghostly shape near the old Siwash Cemetery, but whether there was a connection with the ghost of Dancing Mary is not certain.

## GHOST RIDERS AT ELINOR LAKE

Penticton photographer Gary McDougall has long been interested in the history of the Okanagan Valley and the surrounding area. He has explored many of the region's ghost towns, but only once has he come face-to-face with the actual ghosts.

\* \* \* \* \*

One day in August, 1984, Gary and his father, Harold, had taken the road that skirts remote Elinor Lake, about two miles east of Chute Lake. They had just passed the lake itself when Gary pulled his Jeep onto a side road to have lunch. As they stood beside their vehicle eating their meal, Gary and his father heard the sound of horses coming along the main road. Because trees pressed in on each side of the road, the McDougalls could see the riders for only a few minutes during the time it took the horses to pass the intersection. As Gary and Harold watched idly, five horses and riders came into view. Because of the range of ages, and the similarity of dress, they appeared to be from one family: two middle-aged parents riding with three children who were in their late teens or early 20s.

Gary noticed immediately that their clothing seemed to come from another era. They had on felt hats, long-sleeved shirts with suspenders, heavy wool trousers, and calf-high leather boots. Given the age of the daughter and two sons, it was incongruous that the young people at least were not wearing jeans. On the backs of all five were heavy canvas knapsacks of a kind not used in years. Their mounts, also, were not adorned in the finery often associated with modern trail animals — their plain saddles and bridles made them appear like working horses. Gary observed that not only was the garb and gear old-fashioned, but such clothing must have been very uncomfortable on that hot summer day.

As the lead rider passed, he looked in the McDougalls' direction and appeared surprised. Similar bewilderment crossed the faces of the others as they passed by the side road where the Jeep was parked. Harold greeted the older man, who replied, "Hello," and touched the brim of his hat. In a minute or two all the riders had passed out of sight.

The incident left Gary uneasy. There was something wrong with this apparently insignificant event. Why were the riders dressed the way they were, and why did they seemed so surprised at the chance meeting with Gary and his father? Gary walked the few yards up to the road junction, and looked in the direction the horses had gone. There was no sign of them, even though the road ran straight for some distance and the horses were only moving at a walk. Gary called to his father to come up to the main road and asked him how many horses he had seen.

"Five," Harold responded.

"How many [horses' hooves] is that?" Gary asked.

"Twenty."

Then Gary pointed to the shoulder where the animals had walked. Although his own boots left deep marks, not one hoof print could be seen in the soft sand and gravel of the road margin.

## The Man at the Edge of the Forest

More than 20 years ago, Elsa Fraser and her husband, Ray, built a house on Beaver Point Road on the south end of Salt Spring Island. Beside their dwelling was a small lane that wound through a thick forest of old-growth timber before it reached secluded Weston Lake. Elsa often enjoyed riding her horse, Lad, down this road to visit their neighbours.

Elsa wasn't sure when she first noticed that there was something strange about the spot where the road passed through the forest.

At times, when she took one of her dogs along the road, he would growl and act strangely. Also, when she rode Lad near the spot he often became agitated and shied away.

One day in 1978, Elsa and her seven-year-old son, Jason, took one of their dogs for a walk to the neighbours' house. Dusk had fallen by the time they started for home. As they reached the woods, Elsa suddenly noticed a change in the dog's behaviour. The hackles on its neck rose as it stared toward the trees near the side of the road.

To her surprise she saw a figure leaning against a tree, about 15 or 20 feet back from the road. The young man — she estimated that he was under 40 years old — was short and stocky, with colouring and features that suggested he may have been native Indian. He wore a distinctive, Chinese-made, blue-and-grey checkered flannel shirt of a type that was commonly worn 30 years ago.

Although the figure was solid, Elsa knew instinctively that this individual wasn't a living person. Even more disturbing was the hostility he directed toward her. "He was standing there and glaring at me," Elsa recalled. "I felt such anger from him." She took her son's hand and walked quickly toward their home.

*The Man at the Edge of the Forest.* (Picture drawn by Elsa Fraser)

Despite his anger, she was convinced that the young man wanted her to do something for him, that there was a reason why he had appeared to her by the side of the road. One afternoon several months later, she returned to the place where she had seen him. Although she saw nothing, Elsa had a strong feeling he was nearby. "What can I do for you?" she asked. Suddenly she was overcome by severe stomach pains that forced her to rush away.

A few days later, she went to visit her husband's elderly aunt who lived nearby and related what had happened. "Oh," the older woman said, "it was probably the poor fellow who drowned in Weston Lake." She explained that many years ago a crew was logging several acres on a nearby farm when they decided to take their lunch break at the lake. It was a particularly warm day, and after lunch several of the men went for a swim in the cool water, but one person got into difficulty and drowned before his friends could rescue him. Elsa wondered if the man's body had not been recovered from the lake, or if so, had it not received a proper burial?

Some months later, Elsa enrolled in a workshop called "Women in Their Moons," which was given by a native shaman from Seattle. Much of the day-long program was about the way spirits were viewed within the Northwest Indian culture, which Elsa found fascinating. At the end of the course, she approached the shaman and told her about the man who waited by the side of the road.

"Well, Elsa," the woman said, "it looks like you're the one who has to set him free because he seems to be stuck here. You have to honour him, and maybe that will send him on his way." Elsa, though, doubted that she was the person chosen to perform such an act. She knew little about the beliefs of the Indian peoples.

About this time, the neighbours moved away, and a new person, Mary, took up residence in their house. It was not long before Elsa became friends with her new neighbour and she often stopped by to visit. One day she was surprised when Mary described waking up to see a ghost standing at the bottom of her bed. Although startled, Mary remained calm and told the apparition to leave her house. The spirit immediately faded away.

As she listened to Mary's description, Elsa had no doubt that it was the same man she had seen on the road. The incident added to her feeling that she had failed this earthbound spirit. He had given up on her and turned to her neighbour, but Mary didn't understand. Elsa believed it would be her responsibility to release him. During her research into the beliefs of the Coast Indians, she had discovered that local peoples honoured their dead by hanging ornaments in trees. It remained for her, she decided, to build a memorial to this spirit in order to free him from his earthly bonds.

Elsa collected a few items she felt would be appropriate for the memorial and then made a hanging using fishing line, beach-washed wood, colourful stones and a few bones. When it was finished she went alone to the place in the forest that he haunted, and hung the memorial from one of the lower branches of a tall cedar tree. After performing a short ceremony that she had learned from the shaman, Elsa addressed the spirit of the dead man. "I'm honouring your presence here," she said. "I don't know what else to do to help you, but if this is what you need please take what you want from [the hanging] and please move on to wherever you should go."

The spirit didn't make himself known, but after that she no longer felt his presence in the trees at the side of the road. Mary went away for a time, and when she returned, she told Elsa that the ghost she had seen was gone. Elsa hoped that the lost soul had at last found peace. For Elsa, although the experience was upsetting, it was in the end, personally rewarding. "I felt his anger and I felt his desperation," she recalled, "but I also felt very privileged. He somehow communicated that he needed me to do something for him, and to do it was an honour."

Although the little memorial has endured many years of sun, wind, rain, and snow, to this day it continues to hang in the tall tree at the edge of the forest.

* * * * *

As far as is known, there are three major reasons why a ghost haunts a particular stretch of road. First, and most obvious, the spot is close to where he or she died. Second, as in the case of the young man Elsa saw beside the lane, he was really waiting for someone to help him on his journey beyond this plane. Third may be the situation with the riders at Elinor Lake. For whatever reason, the temporal dimension was distorted, bringing two points of time together at one place. Such happenings are more common than one might suppose. Many of the parks staff responsible for maintaining the Gettysburg Civil War battlefields note that men in historic garb are often seen crossing modern roads. Although no trail exists through the road-side brush, at one time these spots marked the routes taken by the soldiers during their army campaigns.

CHAPTER SIX

# Other Haunts

A lthough ghosts are frequently associated with houses, this is not always the case. As has been seen, these entities from another plane can be found in hotels, pubs, theatres and even on the occasional road. It can be said that no place is out of bounds for ghosts. Here are a few other haunts.

## NOT EXACTLY A SNAPPY DRESSER

The Burquitlam Funeral Chapel at 625 North Road in Coquitlam has long had a resident ghost. The spectre, in fact, predates the conversion of the building to a mortuary.

\* \* \* \* \*

The original building that now forms part of the Burquitlam Funeral Chapel was built in 1924 as a two-storey private residence. In 1964, it was purchased by the Killingsworth family and enlarged to serve as a mortuary. The basement of the home has now been made into a suite, and it is here that the ghost is seen. As is often the case, it is not seen directly, but rather glimpsed from the corner of the eye. Even with only indirect observations, however, there is little doubt in the minds of those who have seen him that his presence is real.

According to funeral director Randy McCormick, stories of ghost sightings go back at least to the 1950s. McCormick, who has seen the ghost many times during the last seven years, describes him — a man in his 50s, about five feet, ten inches tall with graying hair — as not exactly a snappy dresser. He is wearing an odd-coloured yellow-brown sports jacket with mismatched brown trousers, brown scuffed shoes, a dirty white shirt with an unknotted plain brown tie draped around his neck, and a medium-dark fedora of a style popular in the 1940s or '50s. The man's eyes are hidden by the hat brim, but his nose, mouth and clean-shaven chin can be seen.

The apparition is usually first observed in the basement at the bottom of the stairs leading to the main floor. From there he walks through the bedroom to the basement hallway and disappears into the area that is now a kitchen and bathroom. McCormick believes that there was once an outside doorway to this area that was taken out during later renovations. It may be through this now-nonexistent portal that the ghost leaves the house. Where he is going isn't clear, but before the suite was completed this section of the basement was an open space. There is one old report that a woman saw him outside crossing the road in front of the building, but lately he has only been seen inside.

McCormick has seen the ghost so often that he no longer thinks of him as unusual. He said nothing about the spectre to other members of his staff until one Monday morning when an apprentice who was working over the weekend approached him and asked if any other funeral director had been in on Saturday. When McCormick said no, the young man admitted that he had been standing at the top of the basement stairs when he saw someone walking in the suite below. He called down to the person, but there was no answer which, the young man said, was rather "freaky." During coffee that morning, McCormick mentioned his own sightings of the apparition. It was then that other staff mentioned similar experiences with the man in the sports jacket, but, for fear of ridicule, they had kept these incidents to themselves.

Until recently the ghost's behaviour was entirely predictable. Sightings were limited to the basement suite, and no other occurrences, such as the sound of footsteps or a drop in room temperature, were reported. He was seen at almost any time of the day or night. In early June, 1996, however, the ghost ventured from his usual haunt in the basement suite. One day McCormick saw him twice. In the morning, he saw the man standing by the altar in the main-floor chapel. Although all the lamps were off, there was sufficient light coming through the narrow window at one side of the room to illuminate the apparition. There was no question that the ghost was solid, for he blocked the light from the window. Later, McCormick saw him again, this time in the basement laundry room where he was standing by the clothes dryer. "How you doing?" McCormick said matter of factly, and kept walking. There was no reply, and when, seconds later, he stopped and turned around, the apparition was gone.

As in many such cases, there is no hint as to who the spectre is, or why he haunts the Burquitlam Funeral Chapel. Time has erased much of the history of the old building, and it seems likely that these questions may never be answered.

## NIGHT SHIFT

Hospitals are often a person's last link to this material plane, and it seems that earth-bound souls frequently do not move beyond this final place. For this reason, many such sites are haunted by the ghosts of former patients. The story of Douglas, the ghost who haunted Vancouver Hospital's old Burn Unit, which was related in *Ghosts* is a case in point, but there are many other tales associated with health-care institutions.

\* \* \* \* \*

According to the owner of the former Oakherst Nursing Home at 7430 Oak Street, Vancouver, the old structure is not haunted, but this opinion isn't shared by everyone. The building, which was constructed in 1913 as a family residence, was used for many years as a private, extended-care facility. After being closed in the late 1980s, it has frequently been used as a location for motion-picture filming. The derelict old mansion has also acquired the reputation of being the site of many strange happenings.

In the middle of January, 1995, the movie *One Foot in Heaven* was being filmed at the building and as part of his duties, the assistant location manager, Jordan Winter, was required to keep an eye on the set. Although Winter did not stay in the building, he made rounds from a Winnebago parked on site to ensure that the house, which contained expensive film equipment, remained secure.

One night as he checked the building, he heard a noise coming from an upstairs room. As Winter climbed the stairs the sound became more distinct: it was the measured beat of a rocking chair moving back and forth. "I felt freaked big time," he recalled, for he had been through the building not long before and knew that no one could be inside.

During the three days he spent on the site, Winter experienced many strange incidents. On January 17, he was checking the outside of the supposedly unoccupied structure when something caught his eye. The curtains covering one of the windows in the glass gazebo at the rear of the building suddenly opened, as if

*The deserted Oakherst Nursing Home.* (COURTESY OF DIANE BELYK)

someone had pushed them apart from the inside. Then, just as abruptly, they closed again.

The following night, Winter heard what he described as "little noises" coming from the basement. Thinking it might be rats, he went around the rear of the building to investigate. To his annoyance, one of the movie hands had left the door unlocked, which meant that he had to secure it from inside the basement. As he entered he heard other noises: what sounded like "someone moving something or dragging something across the floor," toward the rear of the building. By now it was clear to him that the source of the disturbance was not a rodent. "I don't care how big a rat is," Winter observed. "It's not going to make a noise like that."

Late the next night, he was standing in the rear stairwell when he heard a scream coming from inside the building. The sound was high-pitched, as if it was made by a child or young woman. A search of the premises, however, revealed nothing.

The assistant location manager was not the only member of the movie crew to experience odd happenings. One day, make-up artist Elissa Frittaion was in the gazebo when she suddenly felt someone pushing her. "At one point when I got to the part of the room where my back was to the doorway," she reported, "I felt pressure all the way down my back and [the] backs of my legs. It was pushing me towards the door." Frittaion quickly left the room and returned with hairdresser Mariah Crawley who also experienced a force pushing her. "The more we walked [in the room], the more pressure, like 'Get out, get out'," Crawley said. "You feel like you're intruding on someone's space."

According to the former owner of the nursing home, Patrick Shields, nothing occurred while he was on the premises that would make him believe Oakherst was haunted. Assistant administrator Irene Kellman concurred, but she did recall that at one time a plumber was troubled by the sound of mysterious footsteps.

\* \* \* \* \*

Another health-care facility that appears to have a few visitors from beyond the grave is the old psychiatric institution, Riverview Hospital, on the Lougheed Highway in Coquitlam. Given the anguish experienced by many of the residents during the hospital's long history, one may be surprised that there aren't more ghosts haunting the complex. Most happenings have been associated with the three large main buildings that stand on the brow of a low hill overlooking the Fraser River flood plain: Westlawn, Centrelawn and Eastlawn. While in the 1960s the population of the institution was over 8,000, its gradual phasing out has meant that few patients remain. Wards in Centrelawn and Eastlawn have been gradually closed, and the oldest of the three structures, Westlawn, is entirely empty.

In some cases the "hauntings" can be explained as birds nesting in the attic or a homeless person living in an abandoned building, but not all occurrences can be so easily dismissed. Some time ago, on Ward E-2 in Centrelawn, two nursing staff saw what they described as a sheet floating in mid-air. They called the supervisor, but a search of the area revealed nothing to account for what they had seen.

The adjacent building, Eastlawn, has what many of the staff claim to be a haunted elevator. Despite the fact that until the 1970s, Eastlawn was home to several thousand patients, only one regularly operating passenger elevator connected the building's four floors and attic.

The current elevator has been in service many years, but age doesn't seem a valid excuse for its erratic behaviour. Those on board are taken on a rapid ride to all floors, with the exception of the level they had wanted. That the elevator is unreliable has been long known to staff who have to walk up as many as five floors when it is being repaired, but despite considerable effort, no one has been able to eliminate the problems. In the daytime, when there are others to share the ride, the occurrence is no more than an annoyance. Night, however, is another matter, for staff have also reported a sudden drop in temperature moments before the elevator begins one of its erratic journeys. Unfortunately, like many unexplained electrical occurrences, it is impossible to say for sure that there is a ghost in the machine. "At night though," according to one former staff member, "I would have rather walked up the four flights of stairs to my ward than take that damn elevator."

The Westlawn building has been a prime location for the filming of motion pictures and television shows. The long-running

TV series, *The X-Files*, has frequently used it to stand in for any number of American institutions. With the interior of the building now gutted for asbestos removal, though, it is only the outside that is seen on the screen.

It is not surprising that Westlawn has developed a reputation for being haunted. The well-kept grounds surrounding it stand out in contrast to the grotesque appearance of the building itself. The four-storey redbrick exterior with its hundreds of tiny, iron-framed windows, and the marbled foyer leading into a labyrinth of cramped, dark rooms, are reminiscent of the setting for a Gothic horror.

Despite the many patient deaths that have taken place within Westlawn over the years, it seems to have been the suicide of a staff member who lived in the attic (at one time many of the doctors and nurses were housed on the hospital grounds) that sparked the stories of the Westlawn ghost. The details of the haunting, unfortunately, have been lost, but it is true that despite offers of low-rent rooms, many staff refused to stay in the attic after the man's death. Some years later the area was closed as a staff residence, but nurses on the fourth floor working the evening and night shifts continued to report hearing strange sounds coming from above, as if someone was dragging chains across the floor. Staff were unable to investigate because the door to that area was secured by three separate padlocks. Without the keys, it was clearly impossible for an intruder to get in. Yet, while the sounds continued, the locks on the doors remained secured.

Before Westlawn was gutted, Ken Meier worked as location security during the filming of more than 50 different productions. On occasion, the guard dog accompanying Meier on his rounds would suddenly behave strangely. Once he noted that the animal began fighting with something unseen in a corner of one of the rooms. As it had been trained to do, the dog moved forward to protect Meier from whatever was there. "The spit was flying, there was this ferocious growling and all the hair was standing up on [the dog's] back. He was in deep fighting mode," Meier noted. It was only after the dog was taken from the room that he calmed down. It was common for some security staff to refuse to go into the building alone, or to barricade themselves in their offices for an entire shift.

\* \* \* \* \*

The Gorge Road Hospital in Victoria was first located in Ashnola, the home of one of the daughters of Robert and Joan Dunsmuir. Eventually the old mansion was torn down and another building put up in its place. It is difficult to determine when the stories of ghostly activity began, but according to folklore the spectre wandering the halls and rooms is a nurse.

Some years ago an off-duty Victoria police officer arrived at the hospital to visit his mother. When he approached her room he noticed that a nurse was with her. Not wishing to disturb the person caring for his mother, the man went to the nursing station to ask when it would be appropriate to visit. The nurse at the desk replied that no nurse should have been in the room. She went there herself to check, but as she suspected, the elderly woman was alone. When the officer returned, however, he saw a lady in white standing beside the bed.

On other occasions a white light has been seen moving down the halls. As it approaches a person it apparently increases in size before disappearing. The light is thought to be a harbinger of death for one of the patients.

## THE BLUE LADY

If there are still people who believe that ghosts only inhabit dark, dusty old buildings, the haunting of the Penticton Museum should dispel that notion. The building was constructed 30 years ago and its light, airy design creates an atmosphere that invites exploration of the dozens of excellent exhibits. Yet, despite its outward appearance, there are many Penticton residents who maintain the building was, at least until recently, haunted by the Blue Lady.

\* \* \* \* \*

She has been called either Sophia or the Blue Lady by the staff of the Penticton Museum, but her actual name and identity remain a mystery. That she has haunted a museum may not be so surprising, at least according to curator Randy Manuel. "Some people believe that if a person dies when they're not ready and the spirit is not ready to go to its final resting place, then it stays

*An exhibit in the Penticton Museum where the ghost's presence was felt.* (COURTESY OF DIANE BELYK)

around looking for its possessions." Where better to attract ghosts than a place that is filled with treasures of the past? Although Manuel has not personally seen nor heard anything when he has worked late at the museum, he has often experienced the eerie feeling that he is not alone.

The individuals most familiar with the Blue Lady have been the custodial staff who work alone at night in the building. Ted Lee worked in the museum less than six weeks before he handed in his resignation. "You get strange feelings in certain parts of the building," he notes, "and there's no explanation for it." The feeling that someone was there with him was often so strong it sent shivers up his spine. Lee tried to convince himself that it was Judy, the custodial staff supervisor, whom he had heard enter the building. When he would call out, "Judy, are you here?" though, he'd receive no answer. He would check, only to discover that he was alone.

On one occasion, the custodian heard what he later described as a "desperation voice" coming from one corner of the building.

Believing the sound did not originate from inside, he checked the parking lot outside but he could find nothing to explain the incident. At other times he would catch a glimpse of something out of the corner of his eye, "just sort of a haze," he said, "that drifted over." While the apparition was never fully formed, Lee felt that the presence was a woman.

Another custodian who experienced the eerie happenings at the museum was Linda Wylie who worked there for three years. "In the beginning you try to ignore these things," she reported. "You don't mention it to people because you feel there's a logical explanation. But as time went by, too many things were happening."

Like Ted Lee, Wylie knew she wasn't alone during her shift in the supposedly deserted building. "I'd be walking down the aisles in the museum and I'd hear somebody behind me. I'd hear the footsteps. I'd turn around [but] there was nobody there." At other times she heard a rustling sound, like that made by an old-fashioned dress.

Wylie also noted that, particularly late at night, she'd feel a pronounced temperature drop. "You'd be walking down the aisle [and] it would go from normal temperature to freezing. It was like walking into a refrigerator freezer." She would continue on a few more feet and the temperature would suddenly return to normal. According to Randy Manuel, the museum environment is controlled by an automatic system that turns off the air conditioner after six p.m.: there was no way he could explain the appearance of these sudden cold spots.

One night Wylie actually saw the ghost. She had turned the corner of one of the aisles when suddenly she saw the figure of a woman standing before one of the displays. The shape was hazy and the features were indistinct, but she could see that the woman was wearing a long blue dress. Showing considerable courage she stepped forward toward the figure, but as she approached, it dissolved before her. "To me," she recalled, "it's a friendly spirit, it's not out to hurt anybody. It just wants its presence known."

Unlike Linda Wylie, other custodial staff were not able to contend with the presence of a ghost. It wasn't uncommon for new employees to turn in their keys after only a few days. During an 18-month period before 1992, eight custodians quit.

In 1992, though, the strange occurrences at the Penticton Museum suddenly stopped. The reason, according to Manuel, was that the museum was upgrading its storage area. As he was going through some of the old cartons in the rear of the museum before new shelves were installed, he noted an old wooden Pacific Milk box labelled only "Found on east side of river." Given the age of the box he concluded that it was something collected by his predecessor in the 1920s or '30s. He reached into the container and to his surprise he pulled out a human skull, complete except for the lower jaw. He took the box down and began examining its contents. Inside were other human bones, still coated in what appeared to be river clay. With no information written on the box, Manuel had no idea of the source of this macabre discovery. Packing up the carton, he sent its contents to the provincial forensic lab. When the report came back, it noted that the box contained parts of not one but three bodies, probably that of one man and two women. Any clue as to who these individuals were or when they had died, however, was not forthcoming.

To date the remains have not been returned to the museum, which does not displease Manuel, for since the day the bones were shipped off there have been no further strange occurrences at the Penticton Museum. While the identity of the Blue Lady remains a mystery, her absence has made the operation of the museum easier. "Since the bones have been removed," Manuel observes, "we've been able to keep our custodial staff."

## A HAUNTED COMMUNITY HALL

Squeezed against rugged Belcarra Regional Park on one side and suburban Port Moody on the other, the village of Anmore, with a population of less than a thousand, is an anachronism. The community is only about 15 miles from the heart of Vancouver but, separated from the city by Upper Burrard Inlet, it is in an entirely rural setting. Other than its rustic charm, the village has one other claim to notoriety: the Anmore Village Hall is said to be haunted.

\* \* \* \* \*

Originally built as a private residence in 1916 by George and Margaret Murray, the house by the 1940s had acquired a reputation for being haunted. According to legend, the ghost is said to be that of one of the Murrays' hired hands who hanged himself in their kitchen, or alternately, that of a woman who died from a broken heart after the loss of her child. The building, which also houses the Anmore Village Office, was purchased by the civic government at the time the community was incorporated in 1987.

From the beginning, village clerk Terry Dunlop felt uncomfortable in the building. "I've definitely heard things — it can be quite eerie," he reported in 1989. "I know I can distinguish footsteps and I've definitely heard footsteps."

In May 1988, Anmore hired a second clerk, Don Brown, whose office was on the main floor while Dunlop worked from an upstairs room. As Dunlop recalled later:

> We used an intercom to communicate. I'd hear something and ask him through the intercom if he called me, and he'd say no. He did the same to me. For a while we each thought the other was pulling legs. We were spooked to learn we weren't.

*The Anmore Village Hall.* (Courtesy of Diane Belyk)

Although neither man saw anything unusual inside the building, the most common disturbance was the sound of footsteps. Brown recalled being alone in the building early one morning. "I was just sitting by myself. It was pretty dark, and somebody walked right across the ceiling. Everyone said it must be mice, but they'd have to have pretty big feet."

The hall seemed normal enough from the outside, but Dunlop noted that once the sun went down, there was something strange about the property. "I'd come out of the building into the mist. It would be dark and I'd be groping my way to the car and I'd hear coyotes howling. I tell you, it was spooky."

Currently Anmore's two village clerks are both women. Although the building occasionally creaks and groans with age, neither has experienced anything unusual while working there. Whatever the reason for the haunting, the ghost seems to prefer to make itself known to men.

## WHO'S IN THE CAR?

While ghosts are mysterious entities, individuals are often willing to speculate as to who they were in life and why they haunt a particular place. (Whether these theories are right or not is another matter.) In this case, though, no one has ever offered an explanation of the identity of the ghost or why she appeared in the front seat of an almost-new car.

\* \* \* \* \*

In the autumn of 1986, Maureen Simpson (not her real name) was living in Victoria. Before going to work, Maureen sometimes had to drop off her eight-year-old son, Ron, at the home of his grandparents. One day, the sun had not yet risen when she turned off the street into their driveway. The effect was that her own headlights suddenly illuminated the inside of her parents' late-model automobile, which had been parked facing down the driveway.

Ron said, "Do you see that, Mom?" To Maureen's surprise, in the passenger's seat of the car was the figure of an older woman with dark hair. The person had not expected to be discovered, for there was a look of open-mouthed amazement on her face. A few seconds later she simply disappeared, leaving Maureen and Ron shaking their heads. A check of the car revealed nothing unusual: the vehicle was locked and an intruder would have had no opportunity to slip away.

## CHILLIWACK'S OLD CITY HALL

The small agricultural community of Chilliwack, in the Fraser Valley, seems to have more than its share of ghosts. The Duryba poltergeist, which invaded a small farmhouse a few miles outside of town in 1951 was one of the best-documented occurrences of its type in Canada. In the mid-1960s, the haunting of the Fredrickson house became such a media event that the harassed owners were forced to move away to avoid the unwanted attention of the press and public. The community, though, has another interesting ghost story. According to folklore, the ghost of a Chinese opium smoker continues to walk the corridors of the old Chilliwack City Hall.

*Chilliwack's old City Hall, now the Chilliwack Museum.* (PHOTO BY THE AUTHOR)

Before the 1920s, smoking opium was confined almost exclusively to the Chinese minority in British Columbia. For this reason it was not regarded by authorities as a serious crime, and the occasional police raid on local businesses that were fronts for opium dens seemed intended more to generate cash for the financially struggling civic governments than to "clean up" the practice. However, by 1928, society's attitude toward the illicit substances and the people involved in its use had changed. "Opium eaters" could expect a long prison sentence. One Chilliwack citizen who had been picked up by the police for possession of the drug and taken to the small lockup in the city hall found the prospect of years in prison so disturbing that he used the belt of his sleeping cell mate to strangle himself to death.

While the suicide of a European in the city lockup might prove very embarrassing, the death of an Asian was handled discreetly. Like other British Columbia communities during this period, Chilliwack regarded Chinese people as second-class citizens, and they were denied many basic human rights. The incident received little publicity.

Most City Hall workers regarded the story as nothing more than an interesting tale. For Roy Cromarty, the janitor, though, the building was the site of many eerie experiences. Because he usually worked when no one else was in the building, strange noises could not be attributed to other workers. When Cromarty was working downstairs he was often aware of the sound of footsteps across the upper floor. He would also hear the distinct slamming of doors, but when he went upstairs to check, he never found anything out of place.

In 1976, Esther Allin was given reason to regard the story in a different light. One Saturday when the bylaw-enforcement officer had returned to the office for her lunch break, the building was empty except for Joe, the weekend custodian. As was their practice during their meal, Esther and Joe played cards. During the game they were both aware of footsteps walking along the upstairs corridor. Joe searched the building but he could find no reason for the distinctive sounds. All the doors and windows were locked and there was no way an intruder could have entered without creating a noise. It was noteworthy that the incident occurred on Saturday, when the footsteps were not masked by the sound of other workers. After that, for Esther, Saturdays at City Hall were never the same. It was impossible not to be listening for those measured steps along the upstairs corridor.

In 1980, a new city hall was built and the old structure became the home of the Chilliwack Museum. Director Ron Deman states he has had no encounters with the ghost during his time there. Other building staff, though, remain reluctant to discuss the matter.

## THE HAUNTED STUDIO

Like live stage performances, a recording session in a studio can create a highly charged atmosphere that seems to linger long after the music is over. Some researchers believe that such environments support paranormal activity, and the happenings at Vancouver's Mushroom Studios, 1234 West 6th Avenue, may be a case in point.

\* \* \* \* \*

*Mushroom Studios.* (PHOTO BY THE AUTHOR)

According to Mushroom Studios president Charlie Richmond, nothing has ever been seen at the site, but both artists and technicians have felt as if some unseen presence has been at the recording sessions with them. The ghost is also frequently heard. For some he appears to be humming or singing along with the music, while others claim it is a faint voice in the background during recording sessions. The sound is often heard by a number of people at the same time. On occasion, a voice has come through the monitor speakers when the recording studio was deserted.

While some people have speculated that the sound is coming from the street outside, Richmond notes, "The building is so well insulated that the noise would have to be loud enough to be heard in the entire neighbourhood." And no noise is heard outside the Mushroom Studios' building. The theory among recording engineers is that the ghostly voice enters the sound system through the wiring, but no one can say where it originates.

The notion that the studio was haunted began following the tragic death of Shelley Siegel, the president of Mushroom Records, in Los Angeles in 1978. Siegel, who was only 34 years old, died of a stroke. Charlie Richmond, who knew Siegel, feels that there is evidence to suggest that the Mushroom Studios' ghost is not Siegel. The activities at the studio have so far been very low-key, and Shelley, he recalls, "was anything but subtle."

\* \* \* \* \*

One of the strangest "other haunts," though not in British Columbia, is the Toys 'R' Us store in Sunnyvale, California. A sales floor full of happy children is not the place one might expect to meet a ghost, yet the staff in this relatively modern building have reported strange happenings since 1970. There is some evidence that the ghost is actually that of a pioneer rancher who once owned the land. Hauntings do not always occur in what people might consider the expected places.

CHAPTER SEVEN

# More Haunted Houses

A floating woman, a mischievous little boy and an invisible cat are only a few of the ghosts haunting these houses.

## THE WOMAN AT THE WINDOW

From the beginning, forests have provided British Columbia's men and women with an uncertain living. This is particularly true for the lumber industry where even small fluctuations in wood prices can spell the success or failure of the small sawmills. Regrettably, the skeletal remains of abandoned mills are an all-too-common sight throughout the southern half of British Columbia. One such operation that never lived up to the hopes of its owners was the old Ferguson Mill, near the small community of Cherryville, about 50 miles east of Vernon. A reminder of earlier, more hopeful days, when the mill was operating, is a large, two-storey house that stands across the road from the original Ferguson site. This property has another reminder of the past: it is haunted by the ghost of a woman long dead.

\* \* \* \* \*

118

When John and Linda Kerkkonen, with their two small children, rented the house in the fall of 1971, it had been empty for many months. Built in the early 1950s, shortly before the mill closed, the dwelling was remote and it was often difficult for the owners to find anyone willing to rent it. Moreover, those who moved in frequently didn't stay. The house was not entirely ideal, and John knew that a number of repairs would be necessary before they would be comfortable. The fuse box had been removed earlier so there was no electricity, at least until it could be replaced, and the large wood-and-coal furnace in the basement did not work properly. Despite these difficulties, John and Linda liked the house. The beautiful hardwood floors in the halls, living room and bedrooms were an indication that no expense had been spared during construction. Also, Linda liked the many large windows, which gave the dwelling a cheery appearance.

With winter approaching, Linda's greatest concern was that the property was so isolated. Five-month-old Greg was a sickly baby, and the nearest hospital was in Vernon, more than an hour away. Worse, John worked out of town at a logging camp, and came home only on weekends, so most of the time she would have to manage on her own.

As the Kerkkonens moved into their new home, the season's first snowfall was blanketing the ground. By the time their furniture had been unloaded, John and Linda were exhausted. Long after the children were put to bed the young couple finally retired themselves, much too tired to worry about hanging the curtains in their own bedroom. Privacy did not seem to be a major concern, for their room was at the rear of the house. However, as they began to change for bed by the light of a gas lamp, Linda suddenly noticed the figure of a young woman walking past their window. She wore what seemed to be a white nightgown made from some sort of semi-sheer fabric. Her hair was a rich auburn colour, her eyes dark, and her face strikingly beautiful. Before she passed from view, she turned toward John and Linda and smiled warmly.

The couple looked at each other in astonishment. They had both seen their strangely dressed visitor, but what was the explanation? Had somebody had car trouble on the highway and walked around the rear of the house looking for lights? The person would have had to come up the back steps first, but neither John nor Linda had heard the sound of feet on the stairs nor a knock at the door. They slipped on their coats and went outside, but all they saw were flakes of snow caught in the glow of their lamp.

In the morning they were still mystified. A search of the snow around the house revealed only two sets of footprints from last night: their own. Puzzling also was the fact that their window was six feet above the ground. The lady in white had been visible from the waist up, which meant that she had to be standing on thin air. As they discussed the previous night, John and Linda recalled that she didn't seem to walk so much as float — as if she were as light as a feather. Even more difficult to explain was how she could be seen at all. It had been dark outside and, with the light from the bedroom lamp, it should have been impossible to see anything beyond the room. Yet they realized the woman's form was clearly visible, as if she was illuminated by some inner light. Although the incident was unsettling, John and Linda were not prepared to admit to themselves that the lady at the window had been a ghost.

Some weeks later, however, John met their mysterious visitor again. On this occasion he was in the basement trying to repair the furnace. Although he had no trouble building a good fire, little heat reached the vents on the first and second floors. As he worked at this task, John was suddenly struck by a feeling he was no longer alone. "As I turned around," he said later, "she was standing right there." The auburn-haired lady was looking at him with a contented smile on her lips. As before, she was wearing what seemed to be a nightgown. Overcoming his fear, John stood up and began speaking to her, but the spectre did not reply, and as he moved forward, she began to retreat. "It seemed like she [was taking] steps, but they were so light," John recalled. It was as if she was not really in contact with the floor. When he moved toward her she walked into what had been an old coal bin. Then to his astonishment, she seemed to pass completely through a cement wall at the far end. Severely shaken, he went upstairs to tell Linda what he had seen.

Following the sightings, the ghost used other means to make her presence known. Some of the most frustrating occurrences concerned the frequent disappearance of items around the house. John, who saved stamps and coins, would frequently find them missing from his collection, only to have them turn up later in the most unlikely places. For Linda, who was home most of the time with only the children, the disappearance of an entire package of fancy pink envelopes from her table was particularly annoying. The envelopes were never seen again.

Often the Kerkkonens heard footsteps originating above their heads on the upper floor, as if someone was walking back and forth. When they went upstairs to investigate the sound would stop suddenly. Footsteps were also frequently heard on the stairway leading to the upper floor. Again, no one could be seen. In the living room the drapes sometimes moved, as if someone was brushing past them.

At times John and Linda didn't hear or see anything, but they could sense the woman's presence. At first it was frightening, but gradually they realized their visitor did not wish to harm them. On the contrary, she seemed to want to help, and was particularly drawn to the two children. For infant Greg, the first few months of life had been very difficult. Often he would wake up in the middle of the night in great discomfort, and Linda had to spend a lot of time settling him again. They had not been in the house long before John and Linda noticed a change in their baby's behaviour. While Greg continued to awaken often, he seemed now to settle quickly, so that after a few minutes he would be cooing contentedly in his crib.

For Linda, the presence gradually became a comfort. When John was away during the week, Linda had to keep the driveway clear of snow in case she had to rush Greg to the hospital. This meant that Greg and his 18-month-old sister had to be left in the house alone while she shovelled a path for the car. Often, as Linda worked, she would look up at the living-room window, and the ghost would be standing there looking down at her. When Linda returned inside the children always seemed contented, as if someone had been there looking after them. "I just knew she was there for me," Linda remembered.

John and Linda were not the only persons to see the apparition. People they knew would drive by and later ask about the strange woman standing at their living-room window. One snowy winter evening the Kerkkonens were visited by another young couple, a school teacher and her husband. As the guests sat in the kitchen they saw someone walk past the window.

"Who was that?" the couple demanded.

Fearing ridicule, John and Linda had said nothing to anyone about the ghost. However, since the description given by their guests matched that of the lady in white, there was little choice but to admit the truth. Armed with flashlights, the two couples searched outside in the snow for her footprints, but didn't find them.

The ghost remained a frequent guest at the Kerkkonen home until John and Linda moved away in the following spring. It wasn't the ghost that brought about their relocation. In fact they had become so attached to her that leaving was almost like losing a friend. The reason was simply that the landlord wanted to let the house to a member of his family. In the end, though, the new tenant stayed only one month before moving on to Calgary.

Not until the Kerkkonens had settled into a new house did they tell Linda's father, a long-time resident of Cherryville, about the ghost. The couple wondered if he knew who the ghost could be. The only violent death of a woman in the area, he could recall, was not at the house, but at the old mill site across the road. Sometime in the early 1950s, a young woman and her baby had died in a house fire there. Before giving her own description of

*John and Linda Kerkkonen's haunted house, as it was in 1972.* (COURTESY OF JOHN AND LINDA KERKKONEN)

122

the apparition, Linda asked her father if he knew what the woman had looked like. Yes, he said, he would never forget her. She was a striking young woman with hair the most beautiful shade of auburn.

\* \* \* \* \*

Some years after their experiences at the old mill house, the Kerkkonens paid a visit to their former neighbourhood. The family living in the house at the time, though, were reluctant to discuss whether or not they had had any unusual experiences there.

## THE UNSEEN

While most people think of apparitions as the most terrifying of ghostly manifestations, other unusual happenings may be equally frightening. A secured door that flies open on its own or the sound of an unseen presence walking across a wooden floor can be a very scary experience. In the following two cases, the entities were never seen, but those involved had no doubt that ghosts were present.

\* \* \* \* \*

In 1934, Alfred and Lily Rogers were pleased to find the grey, two-storey house on the corner of Victoria Drive and 13th Avenue in Vancouver. The rent was not unreasonable and the property seemed to fit their needs perfectly. The full-basement dwelling was large enough for the Rogers, their 16-year-old son Fred, their two daughters, Jessie and Ruby, and the family dog, Sport. Included with the house was an additional lot which allowed Mr. Rogers, who was in the wood-and-coal business, to park his delivery truck safely off the street.

The only concern the new tenants had came about the time they moved in, when the next-door neighbour told Mrs. Rogers that nobody seemed to stay in the house long. She didn't explain why this was the case, and Mrs. Rogers regarded it as simply an off-hand remark. Yet it was not many days before they began to wonder if there was indeed an explanation why the dwelling was so often vacant. Family members were frequently aware of a strange feeling. "It was an intense sensation something was watching us," Fred recalled years later. Even the dog was affected, for the fur on Sport's back would sometimes stand on end for no apparent reason and he would begin to growl.

One of the first happenings the Rogers family noticed concerned the turn-of-the-century front door, which had a large oval window set into the frame. Although easy entry could be obtained by breaking the glass, the door itself was solid, with a good bolt mechanism that seemed to lock securely. Yet often in the daytime, the door would be found to have opened on its own. For Mrs. Rogers, who was home alone while Fred worked with his father and the two girls were in school, the behaviour of the door was particularly frightening. The dog, too, seemed to have difficulty with the door. When it opened on its own, the animal would begin to whimper and move away from the entrance hall.

The family wondered whether someone had a key, and was playing a prank by unlocking and opening the door. Such an explanation seemed unlikely, for the large window in the panel provided an excellent view of anyone approaching the house. It happened so many times that it was difficult to believe that anyone could have reached the porch without ever being noticed.

Another explanation was that the wind was pushing against the door with enough force to open it. As the Rogers observed, though, the door was discovered to open not only on stormy days, but in calm weather as well. Also, no matter how hard Fred and his father pushed and pulled it in its frame, the door wouldn't spring open.

Fred was home by himself one day when he had to go down to the basement. He had been there a few minutes when he suddenly heard the sound of footsteps coming up the wooden front steps. Thinking that it might be possible to catch the prankster at last, the young man rushed out through the basement door. "There would have been no time for anyone to avoid me," Fred noted, but to his surprise no one was there.

The two Rogers daughters were particularly upset by the happenings. Both were unable to sleep at night. One Saturday evening, Mrs. Rogers had taken Ruby, her youngest child, to the theatre, while the rest of the family stayed home. A few hours after the two left, Fred, Jessie and their father heard the sound of footsteps climbing up the front stairs. The elder Rogers asked Jessie to open the door for the returning family members, but there was no one on the other side of the door. Something seemed to be there, though, at least judging by the dog's behaviour — Fred noted that the fur on the back of Sport's neck was bristling. Mr. Rogers went outside and searched the front of the property as far as the road, but nothing could be seen.

The last straw for Mrs. Rogers happened some months later when Fred and his father returned from work to find her standing in the back yard. Trembling, she refused to return inside the house, and it was some time before she would tell her story. During the morning the door had opened two or three times on its own, but Mrs. Rogers never could find anyone on the steps. Around noon she was preparing lunch in the kitchen, from where she had a good view of the living-room door. Convinced that the door had been opened by some neighbourhood prankster, she was listening for the sound of an intruder. When she heard the click of the latch she glanced up at the door just as it swung slowly open. As she looked out on the porch, she discovered that no one was there.

Mrs. Rogers refused to spend another night in the house. She took her two daughters and found temporary accommodation. Mr. Rogers gave the owner notice, and a short time later he and Fred loaded the truck with the family possessions and moved.

\* \* \* \* \*

Another haunting that was characterized by what was heard rather than seen took place in Vancouver in 1984. Stephany Grasset and her college-aged son, Stephen, were living in a house on West 52nd Avenue, near the University of British Columbia. By Vancouver standards, the dwelling was old — built not long after the turn of the century. Typical of houses of the period, the front door opened into a narrow hallway that had a set of French doors leading to a large living room. The stairs in the hall connected the main floor with the second level where the bedrooms were located. At the rear of the house, another stairway led from the main floor kitchen to a suite in the basement, which had been leased to a young French student studying at UBC.

This was a difficult period for Stephany: her daughter had recently moved out on her own. The death of Stephany's brother added to her feelings of loss, and to make matters worse Pat, Stephany's roommate, had taken her own townhouse. The large, five-bedroom residence seemed suddenly very empty.

Adding to Stephany's despondency was the death of a young social worker, Carol Smith, a friend she had shared with Pat. Although she had been ill for some time, Carol's death at age 26 seemed tragic indeed, for she was just starting out on her professional career. Although Stephany was able to carry on her normal duties as a nursing instructor, she remained depressed. She had sought the help of a Vancouver psychiatrist, but found the drugs he prescribed only made her feel worse.

One day Stephany was tidying up the bookshelf in the living room when she happened to open a box that contained some of Carol's belongings. Among the books and costume jewellery was one valuable item: a gold signet ring Carol had always worn. For some reason, Carol's parents had not wanted it when they had taken the rest of her things. Stephany had expected Pat to pick up Carol's remaining possessions, but she had not done so. It suddenly struck Stephany that if Pat did not check carefully through the box, she might inadvertently give the ring away with the other, less valuable items. To keep it safe she slipped it on her finger. Given Stephany's emotional state, her concern about the ring was gradually pushed out of her mind until she had all but forgotten that it was still on her hand.

At this period, Stephany's depression had led to sleeping difficulties, and during the night even the faintest sound would bring her back to full consciousness. One evening she was awoken by the sound of the front door opening, which was then followed by the distinctive rattle as the double glass doors leading to the living room parted. As Stephany listened, she heard the rhythmic tap, tap, tap of shoes walking across the hardwood floor of the living room.

Stephany thought it could have been Pat arriving late to pick up something she had forgotten. When Stephany went downstairs, however, the French doors were closed and there was no one there. Puzzled, she returned to bed. From then on the disturbances happened almost every night. The time varied between one and three in the morning, but the pattern was always the same: the front door opened, followed by the rattle of the French doors, then the distinctive tap of shoes across the floor. From her bedroom above, Stephany was aware that the sound always seemed to stop at the bookshelf nearest the dining room, but when she went downstairs to check, nothing was ever disturbed.

Stephany believed that she must be imagining the incidents, but one night in May, after being awakened by the sounds downstairs she went into the hallway and noticed the light was still on in her son's room. Stephany knocked on his door and asked, "Stephen, did you hear that?"

"Yes," he said. "It's just Martine coming home." But Stephany was sure it wasn't their French tenant, for classes were over and she thought the young woman had already left to spend her summer in Europe. To make certain she went down to the basement, but Martine was not there.

Sometime later, Stephany had a house guest, an old friend who now taught at the University of Alberta. During the night, the woman knocked on her hostess' door, asking her if she had heard the noise downstairs. "Yes," Stephany said, "it's my ghost." The woman was apprehensive, but Stephany assured her that the nightly visitor was harmless.

Since her son often worked late at the Frederick Wood Theatre, Stephany found it difficult to remain alone at night. For this reason she asked Sharon, a friend who was then attending UBC, to take one of the extra rooms in the house. Sharon had not been in the house long before she came downstairs one morning and reported that she had been awakened during the night by the rattle of the living-room doors.

Sharon's confirmation was important to Stephany, for it meant that the nightly noises downstairs weren't simply her imagination: three other people had also heard the ghost. What was more, it seemed clear to Stephany that the phenomenon had something to do with her dead friend, for the footsteps always seemed to stop at the bookshelf containing the box that held Carol's books and jewellery.

About this time, Stephany found another psychiatrist, Dr. Erick Leyland, who was a well-known practitioner in the Vancouver area. During one of her sessions with Dr. Leyland, Stephany told him about her haunting. To her surprise, he didn't dismiss the happening as a product of her depression. He told her that he too believed in ghosts. According to the psychiatrist, the only way to stop the happenings was to get rid of Carol's books and possessions, particularly the signet ring. The ring, he believed, meant a lot to Carol, and she didn't want anyone else to have it. He told Stephany it would be better to throw it away than keep it herself.

That evening Stephany disposed of the remainder of Carol's things, including the ring, and the noises were never heard again. As time passed, Stephany's depression lifted, and her life returned to normal. She has never been able to think of those dark days, though, without recalling the rattle of the French doors and the tap, tap, tap of shoes across the living room floor.

## THE PHANTOM CAVALIER

Robert and Juanita Casavant have always wondered why the ghost of an English Cavalier had picked a farmhouse in Surrey, British Columbia, to haunt. It seemed clear that he enjoyed this piece of rural countryside far from his homeland, for he was a frequent visitor.

\* \* \* \* \*

When the Casavants moved into their new house in the spring of 1986, the previous tenant was removing the last of her belongings. After stopping to chat with Robert a moment, she told him that the dwelling had a ghost, and that she had seen it several times. At first Robert didn't believe her story, but he wasn't in the house long before he knew that she had told the truth.

The small, white-and-green clapboard farmhouse on West 60th Avenue in Surrey had been built about the turn of the century. The original house contained only a kitchen and bedroom on the main floor and another room in the attic, but some years later another section had been added.

Robert and Juanita had been in the house only a few days when they noticed that their Siamese cat, Ernie, was acting strangely. "Ernie was like a dog," Robert recalled. "I could call him and he'd follow me everywhere." But the cat refused to take one step into the living room. As soon as he reached the doorway their pet would stop and howl once or twice, and refuse to go farther. Even with offers of food, Robert couldn't coax Ernie to cross the threshold into the room.

Robert, too, felt there was something strange about the house. He couldn't put his finger on it, but something seemed wrong. At times when he entered one of the downstairs rooms he'd feel the hair on the back of his neck begin to rise. Then one evening, two or three weeks after moving in, Robert was sitting in the den watching television when he had the feeling he was being watched. As he looked through the window that opened into the kitchen — the wall had once been part of the exterior of the original house — he was surprised to see a man standing there. "Immediately I bolted out of the chair and ran straight into the kitchen," Robert recalled, "but there was nobody there." He searched the house, including the closets, but there was no sign of the intruder. It didn't make sense because it had taken Robert only seconds to reach the kitchen, and the man had had no time to leave. Moreover, all the doors and windows were locked, so, Robert wondered, how had this person managed to escape?

In the months that followed, Robert was to see the same visitor many times. Usually in the evening, when he was watching television, Robert would glance through the window into the kitchen and see someone standing there staring at him. The apparition looked solid, and seemed to be that of a man in his late 30s or early 40s, who was quite tall — over six feet — and of a substantial weight, although not obese. He had curly brown hair that flowed to his shoulders. What struck Robert as particularly strange was the way he was dressed. He was wearing the costume of a 17th-century English Cavalier: a leather vest over a white ruffled shirt with puffy sleeves, tight, dark-coloured trousers, and brown, knee-length leather boots. Strange also, given the difficult times from which he apparently came — a period of much unrest — the man wore neither a sword nor any other weapon.

At first, when he became aware that Robert had seen him, the ghost would quickly fade away, but as the months passed he seemed to become accustomed to being observed, and would not immediately disappear but remain standing at the window looking back. If Robert moved toward him, however, the spectre was suddenly gone. On most occasions he would materialize in the kitchen, but at other times, when Robert was in that room pouring a cup of coffee or making a sandwich, the Cavalier would appear in the living room, on the opposite side of the window.

While Juanita never saw the ghost herself, the Cavalier had other ways of making his presence known. The couple had been in the house about six months when they were awoken during the night by the television turned up to full volume. After switching the set off, the Casavants went back to bed but several months later it happened again. For the remainder of their stay in the house, Robert and Juanita were plagued every few weeks by the sound of the television suddenly breaking the stillness of the night.

Another incident that was repeated at least three times during the two years Robert and Juanita lived in the house involved a large metal antique frying pan they used to decorate the kitchen wall. Without warning the Casavants would hear a crash coming from the kitchen and find that the frying pan had fallen to the floor. While it was convenient to blame the trucks passing along the road in front of the house, the couple knew that this explanation made little sense. The three-pound pan would be found six to eight feet away from where it had hung, and to travel that far, the pan had to pass over a glass kitchen table without damaging it.

Though the Casavants sometimes found this ghostly activity bothersome, neither found his presence particularly frightening. The identity of this apparition continues to be a mystery. His costume was from an era before British Columbia was settled by Europeans so there seems little likelihood he had a living association with the house.

The Casavants moved out in 1988, and soon afterward the dwelling was demolished. Whether or not the Cavalier continues to haunt the property isn't known.

## LITTLE BOY LOST

Nothing seems quite as tragic as the ghost of a child. According to some researchers, it is common for the unfortunate spirit to attach itself to a dwelling where there are other living children. This is what seems to have happened in the home of one British Columbia family haunted by the ghost of a little boy.

\* \* \* \* \*

The modern condominium complex near Como Lake in Coquitlam seemed ordinary enough, for it was like many others in the area. Yet in the late summer of 1994, when Margot Cummings (not her real name) moved with her three children into their new home, she was faced with many happenings she couldn't explain.

Margot had been living in her unit less than three months when a disturbing incident took place. She had been sitting in the living room with her mother when suddenly she was aware of a child standing in the kitchen. He appeared to be six or seven years old, with dark hair that was long and curly. The figure wasn't entirely solid, but she had no doubt about what she was seeing. The little boy faced Margot, and seemed to be looking right at her, "as if he was letting me know he was there." The boy remained only two or three seconds before he disappeared. Although shocked by what she had seen, Margot said nothing to her mother who had been sitting with her back to the apparition. The older woman found the idea of ghosts unsettling, and Margot didn't wish to alarm her.

After that, Margot noted other strange things. Her cigarette lighter was constantly disappearing only to reappear later. Even though each time she was sure about where she had left it — with small children, she believed she had to be careful with this potential danger — an exhaustive search usually produced nothing. The next day, however, the lighter would turn up in a place she had previously searched.

Like many small children, her four-year-old son, Troy, had an imaginary friend. On one occasion, though, she began to wonder if her son's playmate was entirely a product of his mind. The children had been put to bed for the night when Margot suddenly heard her son's voice calling out. When she opened the bedroom door she saw Troy lying in bed with his eyes open, tugging at his blanket as if it was being held firmly at the foot end. He looked at Margot and said, "Mommy, he won't let me sleep. Tell him to leave me alone."

In the semi-darkness of the room, Margot could see no one else but to settle her son she said aloud, "Let him alone. It's night time. He's got to sleep, now."

The blanket suddenly seemed to come free, and Troy rolled over and said, "Thanks, Mom. Good night." Had the incident occurred anywhere else, Margot would have dismissed it as a dream that had carried on after Troy had awoken, but after what she had seen herself, she felt there might be a more disturbing explanation. Was Troy's friend the same boy she had seen earlier?

The children's bedroom was always a problem, for it was impossible to keep it warm. Even with the thermostat turned up almost to maximum, the room remained extremely cold. While it may have been the result of poor insulation, it seemed strange that the cold was felt in only that one room.

As the months passed other unsettling incidents took place. When she was in other parts of the house, Margot would sometimes hear the doors of her kitchen cupboards slamming shut. After entering the kitchen, she would often find the cupboard that held her plastic containers open, and the contents spilled on the floor. She could find no reasonable explanation. Such actions seem typical of a small child, but it could not have been her own children, because the incidents usually took place at night time when they were in bed. Neither did the family have a dog or cat that could have created these disturbances.

Another site of strange activity was the cupboard containing empty grocery bags. She would sometimes hear a rustling sound coming from the kitchen. When she went to investigate she would find this cupboard door open and the tile floor covered with the bags she had stored neatly away.

Although these occurrences are mildly disturbing, Margot has not been frightened. The little boy's behaviour has seemed more mischievous than malicious. One night in early 1996, Margot had a dream that she was being approached by a formless being. "As the spirit hit my body in my dream, I woke up and I could feel something going through me. I couldn't move for five minutes." Rather than being upset, the young woman recalled only a feeling of peace. Whether or not her dream had something to do with the little boy who frequently plays in her cupboards, isn't clear. Margot, however, is sure that the ghost in the townhouse is no threat to herself or her children.

\* \* \* \* \*

Another story also concerns the ghost of a little boy who haunted a house. In 1978, Heather Grassick, after leaving the beach house (see page 36), rented a two-storey house on Springfield Road in Kelowna. The accommodation was only temporary — she was having her own house built elsewhere in the city and needed a place to stay until it was finished. Although the house Heather rented was old, she felt it was comfortable.

Heather decided to use one of the upstairs rooms as her bedroom. Not long after moving in, she had gone to bed, but was not yet asleep when she opened her eyes and saw a little boy hovering in the air at the foot of her mattress. He was about six or seven years old with long, straight, blond hair, wearing a t-shirt and ordinary-looking trousers. As she watched him he began making faces at her, as if trying to frighten her. Heather, though, found nothing to fear in his antics for, given his age, such behaviour seemed too commonplace to be scary. During the six months she lived there the same little boy appeared in her bedroom on two other occasions, always making the same faces. When he failed to frightened Heather, the spectre simply floated away through the wall.

Since she had been the only person to witness these occurrences, Heather said nothing to anyone. While she was living there, however, she decided to take a vacation, and asked a girl-friend to house sit during her absence. When she returned, Heather entered the front door to find the hide-a-bed pulled out, and her friend's rosary beads on the table. Thinking that the beads were an indication that there was a serious illness in her friend's family, Heather waited anxiously for her return.

When Heather's friend came back, she explained that the beads had served another purpose. During Heather's absence the woman had taken Heather's upstairs bedroom. One night she was awakened by a strong, unpleasant smell, and although the furnace was on, the room was unusually cold. The next day a friend had come over to visit her, and she told him about the incident the previous night. The man, who had apparently some knowledge of hauntings, told her that the drop in temperature and the odour were a sure sign of ghostly activity. Frightened, the woman decided to sleep downstairs, and took out her rosary for protection.

Some time after Heather moved into her own house, the old dwelling on Springfield Road was torn down. Heather has no idea what became of the little boy who liked to make scary faces.

## THE CAT ON THE BED

Houses are haunted not only by the ghosts of people, but of animals as well. In some cases pets remain behind long after they have died. When university student Peter Vanderlugt and his wife Sara and their five cats moved into the small apartment in a converted house on 16th Street in New Westminster in 1993, they may have thought they had enough pets. It soon became apparent, though, that there was sometimes an extra feline presence in their apartment — a cat that was never seen.

The couple had been in their apartment only a few months when one night they felt a cat jump up on their bed. At first they paid no attention but after several minutes Peter and Sara were curious enough to turn over to see which pet had hopped up on the bed. To their surprise there was no cat there. They had heard no sound of the animal jumping to the floor, but believing that they had simply not heard it leave, the Vanderlugts thought no more of the incident.

A year later the couple moved to another apartment across the hall. They had been in their new place about three weeks when one night Peter felt one of the cats jump up on the bed and push against his body. Because it was a warm night, Peter didn't want one of his pets pressing against him, so, with his feet, he pushed it off the bed. A moment later he felt the cat return to its place on the mattress.

Now fully awake Peter sat up in bed, but no feline was at his feet. To his astonishment, however, he could see indentations about the size of cat paws suddenly appear in the bedspread. The action, as he recalled later, was just as if a cat was turning itself around before settling into a curled-up position. Since they had not lost any of their pets during the time they lived in the house, the Vanderlugts believe the ghost cat had probably been a former resident of the dwelling.

## THE WICKER CHAIR

Some people are more aware of psychic forces within their environment than others. When only one person recognizes the presence of a ghost it can lead to tension, as was the case when Brian Evans and his friend Simon (not their real names) rented an apartment on West 12th Avenue in Vancouver.

\* \* \* \* \*

The apartment building was quite ordinary. Like other blocks along the street it was a low-rise structure of 1950s vintage. The suite had a pleasant, lived-in feeling that Brian and Simon found homey. For Brian, its location had the added convenience of being close to his work. Soon after moving in, he returned from work and decided to have a nap on his bed. He had no reason to believe that something unusual was about to happen. The only sounds were traffic noises drifting in from the street, and the occasional footsteps of Simon moving about the apartment. Brian was about to close his eyes when suddenly he was aware of a shadow on the wall: someone was walking by his bed. He turned quickly to face the intruder, but no one was there. By now, the room had become extremely cold. Not surprisingly, he was frightened, for he had certainly seen something. Whatever it was, though, had vanished in the time it had taken him to roll over. When Brian later told his roommate what had happened, Simon scoffed at the story. It seemed obvious to him that Brian must have fallen asleep and had a bad dream.

One night a few weeks later, Brian suddenly awoke with the feeling that someone was watching him. The room was quite dark, but he was nevertheless able to make out a black figure standing beside his closet. In the darkness the form remained unclear, but there was no doubt that it was a man. He quickly switched on his bedside lamp, but the shadowy figure had disappeared. Again, when Brian reported the incident to Simon, his roommate didn't believe him. After that, Brian was unable to sleep in the bedroom without the curtains open to let in the light from a nearby street lamp.

One sunny afternoon Brian arrived home after work to what was supposed to be an empty apartment — Simon was away. However, when he unlocked the door and stepped into the hallway, he was overcome by the feeling that someone was already there. His first reaction was that someone had broken in, but the door showed no evidence of forced entry. From the hallway he could see that the couch, television and two wicker chairs which made up the living-room furnishings were undisturbed. Yet the sensation was so strong that he feared to take another step into the room. Brian turned and went upstairs to a friend's apartment, and together the two men came down and searched the premises. Although they found nothing, Brian couldn't shake the feeling that he was not alone, that some presence was in the apartment with him.

For Simon, this only confirmed his belief that Brian had too vivid an imagination. He didn't believe in ghosts and had experienced nothing unusual since moving in. A few months later, though, something happened that changed Simon's mind.

One afternoon, Simon was sitting on the couch watching television when he heard the familiar crackle of Brian settling into the wicker chair beside him. Engrossed in the television show, Simon didn't look up until some comment struck him as ridiculous. "Can you believe this?" he said to Brian, but he suddenly realized his roommate wasn't there. Brian was away on vacation and Simon was alone in the apartment. Before Simon could deny his senses, the sound occurred again; this time, though, it seemed that a weight had been lifted from the wicker webbing. His ghostly visitor was apparently leaving.

When Brian returned, he was greeted immediately by Simon. "You wouldn't believe what happened," he said. "Who died in this apartment?" For the next several months the crackle of the wicker chair told Brian and Simon that they were not alone. The two men even grew to regard their unseen visitor as a comfortable companion. As they watched television, they'd hear the crackling noise, and know that he had joined them, "You'd look over and you'd sort of smile," Brian recalled, "and you'd get that tingling feeling in your hair and say, 'Isn't this a good show?' " Several months later, though, just as suddenly as it started, the phenomenon stopped.

\* \* \* \* \*

As an interesting postscript to the story, several years later Brian met a former tenant of the block, a person who had occupied the apartment directly above his. When he happened to mention the haunting, his neighbour admitted that similar incidents had occurred in her apartment. Like Brian, she had no idea of the identity of the ghost.

## APRIL VIOLETS

While Randy Manuel never saw the ghost of his grandmother, he had no doubt that she had returned from the grave. Her reason for coming back was clear enough: she wasn't pleased with him.

\* \* \* \* \*

In 1975, when Randy Manuel and his wife, Sandy, moved into the house that he had inherited from his grandmother, it was obvious that the residence was in need of major renovations. The dwelling, on Hansen Street in Penticton, had been built originally in the 1930s, when money was scarce. An examination of the foundation revealed that the house had been built not on concrete but on boulders, and it would be too costly to attempt to replace these inadequate underpinnings. Sadly, the old family home would have to be torn down and a new house built.

Early the next spring, Randy and Sandy began work on removing the exterior of the dwelling. To save money the couple decided to live in the house as long as possible before it was completely pulled down. One day they were in the yard, demolishing an old garage that had been built beside the house. While they were up in the rafters removing boards, they heard the telephone ring. By the time Randy had climbed down the ladder, left the garage, and reached the kitchen, the ringing had stopped — the person on the other end had hung up. Although, given the delay, it was not surprising that he had missed the call, Randy was nevertheless frustrated. Reaching the phone had been difficult, and it was for nothing.

Before returning to the garage, Randy was suddenly aware of the scent of "April Violets," a talcum powder that had been a favourite of his grandmother's. "You could always smell Grandma," he recalled, "before you saw her coming." Randy was suddenly struck by the notion that the elderly lady had returned from the grave, and what was more, "she wasn't very happy about what we were doing." The reason was obvious: it had been her home for many years, and now her grandson was pulling it down.

When Randy returned to the garage he didn't mention the incident to his wife. A few minutes later, though, Sandy asked, "Who was on the telephone?"

"Nobody," Randy said. "By the time I got there, they'd hung up."

"Funny," she said. "While you were in there I had this strange feeling [that I could smell] talcum powder, the kind old ladies wear."

"Really!" he said.

"I had a real creepy feeling your grandmother was here and she doesn't like what we're doing to her house."

Sandy had met her husband's grandmother only once: ten years earlier, when she was only 16 years old. It seemed strange to Randy that his wife had connected the scent of "April Violets" with the former owner of the house.

## OUT OF THE PAST

For many people, an experience with the supernatural is not soon forgotten. This is certainly the case for Alice Kimoff who can still clearly recall several childhood experiences with ghosts.

* * * * *

Until the 1930s, the False Creek area of Vancouver had been one of the most fashionable in the city, but the Depression left an indelible mark there. As the years passed, many houses stood vacant as owners who could no longer meet mortgage payments found other accommodations. But even houses that remained occupied were only faded images of what they had once been. Paint and repairs were expensive, and not many people could afford the cost of upkeep.

One such house was the large, green, two-storey structure near the corner of West 2nd Avenue and Ontario Street. Although the dwelling in its day had been a cut above other homes in the area, by 1935 it had fallen on hard times. When Frederick and Florence Borge, and their four children moved in, it had stood vacant for some years, and the rooms were showing signs of neglect. Upstairs, a community of mice scampered under the vigilant eyes of plaster cherubs set in ornate ceilings, while spiders everywhere wove their traps to catch unwary insects. The once-beautiful gardens that surrounded the property had become overgrown. Still, each spring the cherry trees in the yard put on a magnificent display, and the wild green garden adorned with beautiful pink blossoms offered a vision very different from that of the soot-covered wasteland of the ironworks next door.

Although moving day had been sunny, summer had long passed. The Borge children watched through the window as an autumn wind tore leaves from the cherry trees. The house was well-constructed but, like others of the period, it was poorly insulated and drafty. On the family's first night, the power still wasn't connected, and that evening they sat down to a cold, candle-lit dinner. Everyone then bedded down around the hearth in the living room. For eight-year-old Alice Borge the new house was exciting, but not until the next day did she and her brothers and sister have a chance to explore the residence. As Alice came to know the house, it did not seem entirely welcoming. In fact, there were rooms that were positively scary.

The children did not play in the attic, which seemed to have an unpleasant atmosphere. The room next to the kitchen, which had a rear stairway to the second floor, also had a vaguely unpleasant feel, but Alice found its advantages outweighed the discomfort. The door to it was kept closed to save heat, and because the stairway was rarely used, she found the room a good, quiet place to sit and read or complete her schoolwork. Since her brothers and sister usually avoided it, she gradually thought of the room as her private study.

The Borges had been in the house a few months when one day Alice stayed later than usual in her room. Absorbed by what she was doing, she was suddenly aware that her mother was calling from the kitchen. The pale afternoon light had almost faded as she stood up and walked across the room toward the door. Suddenly Alice knew that she was no longer alone: someone was watching her. "I stopped dead in my tracks when a column of white appeared before me." Alice remembered later. "I knew somehow that it was male, but the most startling thing about it [was] the large, dark, almost black eyes." She moved toward it without fear, but she was stopped by what she described as a "warning light" that burned in his eyes.

Rushing to her mother and father she exclaimed, "There's something white with big eyes!" Frederick Borge went to investigate, but there was nothing to be seen. "Somehow I knew that he would not see it." she recalled later.

This was not the only incident during the Borges' three-year stay in the house. One summer evening Alice was helping her mother sweep the front porch when she happened to glance toward the ironworks next door. A man was standing on a ladder fixed to a bin holding iron rods. The top hat and black clothes he was wearing were old-fashioned, like the apparel of men from the last century. Alice called out to her mother who also saw him, then they quickly went inside.

Frederick Borge was a man with a scientific turn of mind, and he did nothing to encourage his daughter's belief in ghosts. Many years later, though, long after the family had vacated the house, her father admitted having his own experience there. One day he witnessed a man carrying a hatchet going toward the south side of the house. Concerned, he approached the intruder, but before he could catch up, the man walked through the solid wooden wall and disappeared.

Despite indications that the haunting was not entirely benign, Alice, for her part, recalled that the incidents she witnessed produced more curiosity than fear. In one sense, the happenings might have been inevitable. There is an old Scottish belief that a child born on Christmas will see a ghost, and Alice was born on Christmas Day.

## The Ghost Who Disliked Change

Ghost stories always leave more questions than they answer. Such was the case with the Waldo, British Columbia, occurrence. Why the ghost haunted the small house next to the school isn't known, but the entity was not willing to yield control of this dwelling to strangers.

\* \* \* \* \*

It is difficult to find Waldo on modern road maps, but earlier this century it was a booming sawmill town. Its prosperity, as it turned out, was short-lived, for the two lumber companies that had timber rights in the area wastefully exploited the resources, until by 1929, hardly a tree was left standing. However, unlike gold towns, which spring up overnight and disappear just as quickly, lumber communities seem to wither away. The Krag Hotel, which was the centre of Waldo's commercial life, closed ten years after the last mill ceased operation, while the local school remained open at least until 1960.

Waldo's claim to notoriety concerned the 1910 murder of the Krag Hotel's bartender by a disgruntled former employee. Two days later, the killer met a violent end at the hands of a posse. The Waldo haunting, though, does not appear related to either of these tragic events.

When house painter David Willford and his wife, Marian, came down from Fort St. John to spend the summer in the Kootenay district, they couldn't believe their luck. They found a house in the little community of Waldo that was renting for $25 a month which, even at 1957 prices, was considered a bargain. What was more, the small dwelling came completely furnished, including even the linen on the beds and the fishing rods on the walls. For such a rate the Willfords felt sure that they would be able to tolerate the unusual request of the owner who told them not to change anything. "If a window's up," she said, "leave it up. If you don't, it'll be up the next day."

It wasn't long before the couple became aware that their new home was indeed strange. "The house had two bedrooms," David recalled, "but both my wife and I had an uncomfortable feeling in one of them. I can't explain it today. But we decided not to use that bedroom."

A few days after moving in, the Willfords had spoken with local residents who revealed the dwelling was haunted. According to the postmaster, the house was occupied by the ghost of an elderly man who had lived there many years ago. One story told by a neighbour concerned a former tenant who worked out of town, and came home one weekend to discover a note from his wife. She told him that she was staying elsewhere, and that she wouldn't spend another night alone in the dwelling.

David and Marian needed little convincing that they shared the house with something that was beyond normal understanding. In the late evening, an inexpensive mantel clock would strike the hours even though its internal mechanism had been removed. This was frequently followed by the inside doors closing, and the windows shaking. "Sometimes tremors are blamed for door-closing and window-rattling," David recalled. "We wanted to make sure that wasn't the problem. But nobody in the neighbourhood was using explosives and there were no reports of earthquakes." Nor could a draft be responsible for the happenings, since the heavy, old-fashioned doors did not close easily.

Everything within the house had to be left the way they had found it, for change, it seemed, was not tolerated. If the Willfords happened to leave their clothing on one of the chairs at bedtime, they would wake up in the morning to discover the items placed on the floor. If they closed the bathroom window, which had been partially open when they moved in, next day they would find it returned to its former position. It was not that the ghost was particularly neat. Books that had come with the house were frequently moved, and papers in the desk were riffled, leaving Marian to speculate that the presence was searching for something long lost. Although these happenings were often disconcerting, the ghost never displayed malevolence toward them, and furthermore, given the reasonable rent, the couple decided that they could put up with the strange happenings .

In September, the Willfords returned to Fort St. John and the house was rented to a young couple who had taken teaching assignments at the local school. For whatever reason, the new renters ignored the advice of their landlady and changed the furniture to suit their tastes. The result, so the Willfords were told by neighbours later, was disastrous. One evening the couple was so upset by what was happening in their house that they left and refused to return.

## MRS. FINLAY

Although an uncommon occurrence in the spirit world, place-haunting ghosts sometimes become attached to people. This was what happened with a presence who sometimes visited a young woman after she had moved away from the haunted house.

\* \* \* \* \*

When Leslie and Brian Simmons (not their real names) bought a house in the Cowichan Valley in the late 1980s, the residence was quite new. The former owner, Donald Finlay (not his real name) had sold the property after his wife died. Before the Simmons had moved in, the house seemed normal enough, but they were hardly settled when Leslie began to notice something strange. Mr. Finlay had given Leslie his wife's old Singer sewing machine, which Brian set up in the basement. "I [would be] using her sewing machine," Leslie recalled, "and would feel somebody there — not scary, not cold, or anything like that — just like someone was walking into the room without you looking. She would just wait and watch."

As the Simmons children became older and began using the basement as a playroom, Leslie could feel Mrs. Finlay watching them too. It seemed to Leslie that she, her husband and children were more like guests in Mrs. Finlay's house and that at first the woman was not entirely comfortable in their company. Also, it seemed that Mrs. Finlay preferred that her presence not be made known to other members of the household. Leslie tried to stop looking over her shoulder when she sensed the woman enter the room because she was convinced Mrs. Finlay didn't like that.

Gradually though, the woman seemed to accept the new people living in her home. It was at this point that the ghost's behaviour started to change. Instead of trying to remain undetected, Mrs.

Finlay began making her presence known. Items the Simmons had left in the basement suddenly would be missing. "We'd be looking for things [we knew] had been there a little while before," Leslie recalled. But they couldn't be located.

At other times, Leslie and Brian would be sitting in the living room watching television when they would suddenly hear a noise coming from the basement. When they went downstairs to investigate, they would find the hot-water faucet in the shower stall turned on full, so that a cloud of steam was rising toward the ceiling. Eventually, it was not only the shower that mysteriously turned on by itself. Sometimes the faucet in the bathroom sink would also be running. The Simmons noted that it was always the hot-water taps that were turned on, never the cold.

The presence of Mrs. Finlay was always difficult for Brian to accept. Unlike Leslie, he didn't believe in ghosts. One evening, however, Brian was sitting in the living room when he turned to Leslie and said, "I could have sworn somebody was standing at the top of the stairs." For Leslie the incident underlined what she already knew: Mrs. Finlay was no longer content to simply remain in the basement. On one occasion Leslie was outside pruning a rose bush when she was conscious of Mrs. Finlay standing there watching her. It was not that Leslie was uncomfortable with the haunting. It seemed that Mrs. Finlay was protective toward her and her family, and for that reason she felt the presence of the ghost was reassuring.

Mrs. Finlay's attitude seemed to change, though, when the Simmons bought a new house a short distance away. On the morning of the move, Leslie was alone in the old house as Brian took a truckload of furniture to their new place. Leslie was standing in the basement recreation room, which she had used as her sewing room, packing a few items in boxes. Suddenly she was aware that Mrs. Finlay was beside her and that the ghost was very angry. The presence settled upon Leslie like a weight. It was clear that the woman didn't want to lose the family she had grown to know. Leslie attempted to reassure her, but to no avail. Mrs. Finlay's anger was almost palpable.

When Brian returned, Leslie called to him to meet her downstairs. After he came into the recreation room, his eyes opened wide. "Let's get the hell out of here," he said quickly. Two days later, when they felt Mrs. Finlay might have calmed down, the couple returned to pick up the remainder of their belongings.

Although Leslie has not been the only member of her family to experience Mrs. Finlay's presence, she feels that, given the bond they established over the years, the woman is her personal ghost. Before leaving their former home, Leslie had told Mrs. Finlay that she was not moving far away. The ghost has apparently taken this news to be an invitation to visit, although Leslie feels her guest is a weak presence away from her own haunt and does not stay long. One of Mrs. Finlay's favourite tricks has been to hide books Leslie wishes to lend to other people. When she comes to pass them on they no longer can be found, only to turn up unexpectedly a few days later.

\* \* \* \* \*

While haunted houses are more common than most people probably realize, a fair question might be why are there not more such places? Certainly, if every house where a death occurred was haunted, the world would be awash in ghosts. Some researchers maintain that ghosts are associated with sudden, violent death, but even here the evidence is far from overwhelming. Many houses that have been the scene of terrible crimes later show no evidence of haunting.

CHAPTER EIGHT

# Visitors and Guests

Death does not always close the book on a life. Sometimes the deceased person comes back to friends or relatives with a message from beyond the grave.

## GRAN'S GHOST

Diabetes had cost Eileen Keeping both legs and for the last several years of her life she was confined to a wheelchair. Her final few months were spent in a hospital where she was surrounded by her children and grandchildren. For nine-year-old Garrett Keeping, the death of Grandma had been tragic — he and his grandmother had been particularly close, but he settled back into the usual routine of school and home. The year after Eileen Keeping's death, Garrett, his mother Maggie, and his little sister, Kayla, moved into a new dwelling.

From the beginning, Maggie Keeping felt there was something strange about the two-storey house on Mara Drive in Coquitlam. Although it was less than ten years old, the floors already squeaked. The sounds could not be dismissed simply as the house settling: during the evening after Kayla had been put to bed and she and Garrett sat in the living room watching television, they would hear the sound of footsteps in the upstairs bedrooms. Yet there was no other adult in the house. Maggie has never been able to find a reasonable explanation for the happenings.

On other occasions she and Garrett would be aware of the gentle scent of perfume in the air — the same kind her mother almost always wore. Although the house had modern, double-insulated windows to prevent draft, Maggie would sometimes notice the drapes in the living room moving.

Garrett also had strange experiences in the house. Once, when he was upstairs and the others in his family were down on the main floor, he closed the window in his room, only to feel a draft several minutes later. When he got up, he was surprised to see that his window was open again. No one else had been in his room. Several times, he caught sight of his grandmother out of the corner of his eye. When he looked around, though, no one was there.

One evening in the spring of 1995, Garrett was in his room on the second floor when he thought he glimpsed his grandmother, in her wheelchair, pass along the hallway. Knowing this to be impossible, he assumed it must have been his little sister who had walked by. She would have been the same height as his grandmother in her chair. When he found his mother in her bedroom, "Mom," Garrett said, "has Kayla been by my room?"

"No," Maggie answered. "She's been here with me."

Still unsettled, Garrett decided to go downstairs, but he had hardly reached the bottom step when he saw the ghost of his grandmother, standing only a few feet away, looking at him. What amazed the boy was that now she had both her legs. He remembered her only as a person confined to a wheelchair. Her body was solid, except for the feet, which seemed to fade away. What struck him, also, was that the figure before him seemed to be illuminated by an inner light. It was as if she glowed.

As he stood transfixed, she raised her arm and motioned him to come to her. "I miss you," she said. Garrett would later describe her voice as completely normal.

Garrett was too frightened to move. Instead he began calling out to his mother that Grandma was right there with him.

In response to the fear in her son's voice, Maggie Keeping came quickly downstairs. Garrett was standing staring into what appeared to be an empty room.

"Grandma's right here, can't you see her?" he said.

Maggie had to tell her son that she saw nothing.

"Mom, I can prove she is here. Grandma, go give Mother a hug." It was as if the temperature suddenly dropped several degrees. Maggie shivered involuntarily. By now she was crying. She staggered down the hall to the family room. A few minutes later Garrett entered with, so he said, his grandmother.

For Garrett the whole affair was both frightening and frustrating. What he was saying was upsetting to his mother, but he was only telling the truth. "Why can't Mom see you like I can?" he asked his grandmother.

"Because I don't want to make her upset," came Mrs. Keeping's reply.

By now Maggie, through Garrett, was putting questions to her mother. After a while Maggie asked if Mrs. Keeping ever visited her where she worked as a supermarket clerk.

"No," he said, "she doesn't like it because it's too loud and noisy."

Soon after that Garrett looked away, and when he turned back to where his grandmother had been sitting she was gone.

That evening Maggie phoned her older sister, Jackie, and told her what had happened. When she mentioned what Garrett had said about the supermarket, her sister exclaimed "Don't you remember? Mother never liked going to your store. It's too big and noisy." Since it had been four years since her mother's death, it would have been unlikely for Garrett to remember such a trivial detail when even she couldn't recall it at first. Garrett still feels uncomfortable sometimes going upstairs alone. Ghosts can be frightening, even when they're the spirit of someone close to the heart.

## A FAMILY VISIT

Albert Nelson Dunsmore died in 1956, when his daughter, Marilyn, was nine years old. While the loss was severe, Marilyn, her brother John and her mother, Jean, had to go on. Eventually Marilyn's mother remarried, and Marilyn adjusted to the new family situation well: she was very fond of her stepfather and adored her new sister, Janelle. Although she never forgot her natural father, memories of him began to fade.

One night, when Marilyn was 16 years old and living in the family home in Princeton, she retired to bed as usual. The room was particularly dark; no light entered from the curtained window or under the closed door. As she lay in bed with her eyes open, she noticed that the darkness seemed to have a grainy texture, like coarse sandpaper. As she watched all these individual molecules of sand seemed to come together at the foot of her bed. Standing there in the darkness was the form of a man. By now the teenager was very frightened, for it was all too real to be a dream. As she looked on, it suddenly occurred to her that the image she was seeing was that of her father, Albert Dunsmore. The figure began moving around the end of the bed toward her. As he came closer, he reached over and pulled the chain on the lamp beside her bed. Instantly, the room was flooded with light, and the ghost was gone.

Shaken, Marilyn got up and went downstairs and poured herself a glass of milk. A few moments later, her mother appeared from her own bedroom. Marilyn told her about the incident a few moments before. Although she seemed surprised, the older woman said little and after a few minutes Marilyn got up and returned to bed.

Five years later Marilyn was completing nurses' training in Vancouver, when she returned home for a visit with her fiancé Elvin. One evening Marilyn, her mother, and Elvin were sitting around the kitchen table talking about ghost stories. Marilyn began retelling the story of the figure at the foot of her bed, when her mother suddenly stopped her. "I didn't want to scare you that night," the older woman began, "but I woke up and felt that he was in [my] bedroom." When she arose and went to the kitchen and found her daughter, she was shocked to hear Marilyn's story.

That both women shared the belief that Albert Dunsmore had returned from the other side that night was indeed strange. But why that particular night, they wondered. It was no one's birthday or anniversary. As far as they knew, there was no reason why he should have come back then.

\* \* \* \* \*

On the highway between Princeton and Kamloops, Marilyn has frequently had another unusual experience. Not far from MacKenzie Lake there was a spot where Albert Dunsmore used to train his hunting dogs. The area was so closely identified with the man that the small body of water there is still called Flight Lake by the locals, after one of her father's retrievers.

On rainless days when Marilyn drives past the lake, her windshield wipers often turn on suddenly, making two passes over the dry glass before stopping. No one has ever discovered a mechanical problem with the wipers, and indeed, they have never turned on by themselves on another stretch of road.

## I STOPPED BY JUST TO SAY THANKS

Several years ago, Randy and Sandy Manuel were living in their new house on the property willed to him by his grandmother, when he had an encounter with someone from beyond the grave. Oddly, Randy's spirit visitor was not a relative nor even a close friend, but simply a man for whom he had done a small kindness.

\* \* \* \* \*

At one time Randy had developed an interest in 16-mm motion-picture photography, a hobby shared by Jack, who ran a photographic business in the city. Because he couldn't yet afford the cost of a projector, Randy often visited Jack to use his machine.

During this time Jack became ill with cancer, and as the months passed his condition worsened. During one of Randy's visits, Jack happened to mention that his father had been one of the area's pioneers in motion-picture photography, and he had been left a sizable collection of this work. Knowing Randy's interest in history, Jack asked if he would like to duplicate and edit the reels as a record of the area. Randy was more than pleased to undertake the task.

About the time Randy finished the job, Jack was taken to the hospital in serious condition. Given the fact that Jack had not seen the finished work, Randy received a call from his family asking that he set up the equipment in the hospital room so that Jack could see the finished product before he died.

One day Randy toted the heavy projector into Jack's hospital room and ran the films he had compiled. Jack seemed pleased with the results, although by now he was heavily sedated to lessen his pain.

Jack died in the early spring, and Randy quickly forgot this episode, until one morning when he was awakened early by the weight of something pressing on the foot of his bed. "There was Jack sitting in his hospital garb." As Randy became fully awake, the other man stood up and said, "Thanks for showing me the stuff." Then he turned quickly and walked from the room.

What surprised Randy was that he had only known Jack casually. All they had in common was their interest in motion-picture photography. Was it really necessary to return from death to acknowledge this simple act of kindness? Randy doesn't know.

* * * * *

People-haunting ghosts, like those described in this chapter, usually do not remain earth-bound long, and their visits are limited to one or two brief appearances. Often, the reason for their return is understood more clearly than the appearances of other ghosts. For example, in the case of Lieutenant James Sutton, who was murdered by some of his classmates at the naval academy in Annapolis, Maryland, in 1907, the purpose for his return was to tell his mother that he did not commit suicide as the academy claimed. On the night of his murder, James' mother was visited by his apparition who said, "Momma, I never killed myself ... " He went on to give the details of his death. Although the navy failed to change the verdict of its investigation, a lot of evidence was gathered supporting James' claim that he had been murdered.

The reason that many visitors return briefly, though, is often less dramatic. They want to say a goodbye to friends and family.

# ENDNOTES

## Preface

viii "as if ...": personal interview with C.J. Elliot (pseudonym), February 19, 1996; all following quotes are from the same source.

## Introduction: On the Nature of Ghosts and Their Haunts

xiv "My first ...": quoted in Arthur Myers, *The Ghostly Register* (Chicago: Contemporary Books, 1986), p. 243.

xiv "Wagon wheels ...": quoted in *ibid*.

## Chapter One: Historic Haunts

### Haunted Hat Creek Ranch

3 "John West ...": *British Columbia Mining Journal*, September 28, 1895.

4 "Help me ...": quoted in telephone interview, August 13, 1996. Interviewee's name withheld.

4 "See Mommy ...": quoted in personal interview with Susan Forceille, July 6, 1996.

6 "the hair ...": personal interview with Kristina Grant, July 6, 1996.

7 "It's like ...": personal interview with Susan Forceille, July 6, 1996.

7 "Something happened ...": personal interview with Nels East, July 7, 1996.

### Mrs. Hayes

10 "No ...": quoted in personal interview with Barry Schanehorn, July 7, 1996; all following quotes are from the same source.

### The Mouse Woman of Kitselas Canyon

12 "The presence ...": personal interview with Ian McEwan (pseudonym), November 14, 1996.

### The Legend of Chute Lake's Phantom Piper

14 This story was related to the author by Gary McDougall during a telephone interview, September 11, 1996.

## Chapter Two: Haunted Houses

### Mary's Ring

23 "I have ...": quoted in personal interview with Victor Oulton (pseudonym), April 15, 1996, and the following four quotations.

26 "I feel ...": transcribed from videotape in the possession of Victor and Pamela Oulton

(pseudonyms), recorded March 6, 1995; all following quotes are from the same source.

### Haunted Briarwood

29 "Get down ...": personal interview with Sharon Seymour, September 7, 1996; all following quotes are from the same source.

### The Neighbour

36 "You just ...": quoted in personal interview with Lorne Briere, November 12, 1990.

### The Man in the Plaid Shirt

37 "Who's in ...": quoted in telephone interview with Heather Grassick, October 15, 1996; all following quotes are from the same source.

### The Choking Man

38 "a-hough": quoted in G.E. Mortimore, "All Aboard," Victoria *Daily Colonist*, May 26, 1956, p. 2

### Do Not Disturb

40 "That's enough ...": personal interview with Anne Edwards, May 29, 1997; all following quotes are from the same source.

**Chapter Three: Haunted Theatres**

**The Vogue Theatre**

45 "I don't ...": *West Ender*, October 27, 1994, p. 4.

45 "I was ...": Bill Allman interviewed by Mark Forsythe, *Afternoon Show*, CBC Radio, Vancouver, October 28, 1994, and the next quote.

47 "The only ...": personal interview with Shane McPherson, December 4, 1995, and the next quote.

49 "This theatre ...": Vicki Gabereau, *Vicki Live at the Vogue*, June 6, 1997.

**The McPherson Playhouse**

52 "There's somebody ...": quoted in personal interview with Tom Heemskerk, November 14, 1996, and the following four quotations.

53 "We do ...": personal interview with Blair Morris, November 14, 1996, and the following two quotations.

**The Royal Theatre**

56 "At the end ...": personal interview with Blair Morris, November 14, 1996, and the next quote.

56 "There was ...": personal interview with Tom Heemskerk, November 14, 1996, and the next quote.

58 "Nobody ...": personal interview with Harvey Ratson, November 14, 1996.

**The Sagebrush Theatre**

59 "It's basically ...": telephone interview with David Ross, August 23, 1996.

59 "It's generally ...": telephone interview with John Reilly, August 23, 1996.

60 "Hey Albert ...": *Kamloops Daily News*, October 31, 1989, pp. A1, A13.

60 "Some . .": *ibid.*

62 "I just ...": *ibid.*

63 "If we ...": telephone interview with David Willford, October 29, 1996.

**The Towne Theatre**

64 "At the same ...": personal interview with Matt Huebner, September 7, 1996.

**Chapter Four: Haunted Hotels and Pubs**

**The Haunted Yew**

70 "It wasn't ...": personal interview with Karen Fontain, July 2, 1996; all following quotes are from the same source.

**Slim and His Dog**

73 "just to make ...": telephone interview with Patty Grotke, October 14, 1996, and the next quote.

73 "In the office ...": telephone interview with Theresa Watkins, October 8, 1996.

74 "Slim ...if you've ...": telephone interview with Jessie Schrader, October 8, 1996.

75 "Sometimes ... I've ...": personal interview with Maryann Rogodzinski, September 24, 1996.

76 "Sit down.": quoted in personal interview with Blair Gelhorn, April 25, 1997.

77 "There are things ...": telephone interview with Al Sholund, November 7, 1996.

**The Face at the Window**

79 "Out to here ...": telephone interview with Ramona Harper (pseudonym), February 14, 1996.

**Friday**

82 "It looks ...": personal interview with Carol Brodie, September 5, 1996, and the following two quotations.

**Susie Woo**

84 "Any time ...": Vancouver *Province*,

October 26, 1986, p. 29.

84 "When I …": telephone interview with Mark Whyte, August 19, 1996.

The Haunted Four Mile House

86 "All right …": personal interview with Wendy Haymes, November 15, 1996; all following quotes are from the same source.

Chapter Five: Haunted Highways

The Phantom of Highway 1

90 "Pull over …": telephone interview with Janice Bradley, October 10, 1996, and the following two quotations.
91 "A marriage …": *Ashcroft Journal*, December 22, 1900, p. 9.

The Lady in Black

92 "I was coming …": quoted in Victoria *Times Colonist*, November 26, 1989, p. A3; all following quotes are from the same source.

Ghost Riders at Elinor Lake

96 "Hello …": quoted in telephone interview

with Gary McDougall, September 11, 1996; all following quotes are from the same source.

The Man at the Edge of the Forest

97 "He was …": telephone interview with Elsa Fraser, May 16, 1997; all following quotes are from the same source.

Chapter Six: Other Haunts

Not Exactly a Snappy Dresser

103 "How you …": personal interview with Randy McCormick, June 18, 1996.

Night Shift

104 "I felt …": Vancouver *Province*, January 30, 1995, p. B3, and the following four quotations.
106 "At night …": telephone interview, August 29, 1990. Interviewee's name withheld.
107 "The spit …": *Tri-City News*, February 7, 1996, p.15.

The Blue Lady

108 "Some people …": The material for this story is based on a personal interview with

Randy Manuel on September 6, 1996, and an undated television interview with Randy Manuel, Ted Lee, and Linda Wylie that is in the possession of the Penticton Museum.

A Haunted Community Hall

112 "I've definitely …": Coquitlam *Now*, October 29, 1989, p. 1; all following quotes are from the same source.

Who's in the Car?

113 "Do you …": quoted in telephone interview with Maureen Simpson (pseudonym), March 5, 1996.

The Haunted Studio

117 "The building …": telephone interview with Charlie Richmond, December 4, 1996, and the next quote.

Chapter Seven: More Haunted Houses

The Woman at the Window

120 "As I …": personal interview with John Kerkkonen, November 12, 1990, and the next quote.
121 "I just …": personal interview with Linda

Kerkkonen, November 12, 1990, and the next quote.

## The Unseen

124 "It was …": telephone interview with A.C. Rogers, October 7, 1996.

124 "There would …": letter from A.C. Rogers to the author, n.d.

127 "Stephen, did …": personal interview with Stephany Grasset, June 27, 1996; all following quotes are from the same source.

## The Phantom Cavalier

128 "Ernie was …": telephone interview with Robert Casavant, April 15, 1996; all following quotes are from the same source.

## Little Boy Lost

131 "as if …": telephone interview with Margot Cummings (pseudonym), February 19, 1996; all following quotes are from the same source.

## The Wicker Chair

136 "Can you …": quoted in personal interview with Brian Evans (pseudonym), March 28, 1989; all following quotes are from the same source.

## April Violets

138 "You could …": personal interview with Randy Manuel, September 6, 1996; all following quotes are from the same source.

## Out of the Past

140 "I stopped …": Alice Kimoff, *Vancouver Sun*, October 31, 1994, p. 6; all following quotes are from the same source.

## The Ghost Who Disliked Change

141 "If a …": telephone interview with David Willford, October 29, 1996.

141 "The house …": quoted in Sheila Hervey, *Some Canadian Ghosts* (Toronto: Simon and Schuster, 1973) p. 16.

## Mrs. Finlay

143 "I [would be] …": transcript of an interview with Leslie Simmons (pseudonym) by Mike Ballantyne of the British Columbia Folklore Society, October 26, 1995, n.p.; all following quotes are from the same source.

## Chapter Eight: Visitors and Guests

## Gran's Ghost

147 "Mom …": quoted in personal interview with Maggie Keeping, March 5, 1996; all following quotes are from the same source.

## A Family Visit

149 "I didn't …": quoted in personal interview with Marilyn Dunsmore Strilchuk, October 5, 1996.

## I Stopped By Just to Say Thanks

151 "There was …": personal interview with Randy Manuel, September 6, 1996.

151 "Momma I …": quoted in Daniel Cohen, *The Encyclopedia of Ghosts* (London: O'Mara Books, 1989), pp. 109-91.

SOURCES

BOOKS:

Akrigg, G. P. V. and Helen B. Akrigg. *British Columbia Chronicle, 1847-1871*. Vancouver: Discovery Press, 1977.

Auerbach, Loyd. *ESP, Hauntings and Poltergeists: A Parapsychology Handbook*. New York: Warner Books, 1986.

Christensen, Jo-Anne. *Ghost Stories of British Columbia*. Toronto: Hounslow, 1996.

Cohen, Daniel. *The Encyclopedia of Ghosts*. London: O'Mara, 1989.

Columbo, John Robert. *Haunted Toronto*. Toronto: Hounslow, 1995.

—. *Mysterious Canada : Strange Sights, Extraordinary Events, and Peculiar Places*. Toronto: Doubleday, 1988.

Finucane, R. C. *Apparitions of the Dead: A Cultural History of Ghosts*. Buffalo, New York: Prometheus, 1984.

Green, Celia and Charles McCreery. *Apparitions*. London: Hamish, 1975.

Hervey, Sheila. *Canada Ghost to Ghost*. Toronto: Stoddart, 1996.

—. *Some Canadian Ghosts*. Toronto: Pocket Books-Simon and Schuster, 1973.

Innes, Brian. *Ghost Sightings*. London: Brown Books, 1996.

Lindley, Charles. *Lord Halifax's Ghost Book*. 1936; rpt. London: Fontana-Collins, 1968.

McKelvie, B.A. *Fort Langley: Birthplace of British Columbia*. Victoria: Porcepic Books, 1991.

MacKenzie, Andrew. *A Gallery of Ghosts*. New York: Taplinger, 1973.

—. *Apparitions and Ghosts*. London: Arthur Baker, 1971.

—. *Hauntings and Apparitions*. London: Heinemann, 1982.

Myers, Arthur. *The Ghostly Register*. Chicago: Contemporary Books, 1986.

Ormsby, Margaret. *British Columbia: A History*. Toronto: Macmillan, 1958.

Rogo, D. Scott. *An Experience of Phantoms*.

New York: Taplinger, 1974.

Skelton, Robin and Jean Kozocari. *A Gathering of Ghosts: Hauntings and Exorcisms from the Personal Casebook of Robin Skelton and Jean Kozocari*. Saskatoon: Western Producer Prairie Books, 1989.

Sonin, Eileen. *More Canadian Ghosts*. Toronto: Pocket Books-Simon and Schuster, 1974.

Smith, Barbara. *Ghost Stories of Alberta*. Toronto: Hounslow, 1993.

MISCELLANEOUS:

British Columbia Archives and Records Service "Hat Creek Ranch." Unpublished report, n.d.

British Columbia Folklore Society Mike Ballantyne, comp. "Ghosts in the Cowichan Valley," Transcription, 1995.

# Sources

NEWSPAPERS:

*Ashcroft Journal*
*British Columbia Mining Journal*
Chilliwack *Progress*
Coquitlam *Now*
*Kamloops Daily News*
*Tri-City News*
*Vancouver Courier*
Vancouver *Province*
*Vancouver Sun*
*Victoria Daily Colonist*
Victoria *Times Colonist*
*West Ender*

INTERVIEWS:

Esther Allin
Bill Allman
John Alvero
Meco Alvero
Janice Bradley
Audrey Briere
Lorne Briere
Carol Brodie
Bill Cameron
Robert Casavant
Margot Cummings
  (pseudonym)
Phil Dubroy
Nels East
Larry Eastick
Anne Edwards
Randy Edwards
C.J. Elliot (pseudonym)
Brian Evans (pseudonym)
Brandy Fitzpatrick
Karen Fontain
Susan Forceille
Elsa Fraser
Blair Gelhorn
Kristina Grant
Stephany Grasset
Heather Grassick
Patty Grotke
Ramona Harper
  (pseudonym)
Wendy Haymes
Tom Heemskerk
Nicole Henzel
Matt Huebner
Holly Jackson
Laurie James
Garrett Keeping
Maggie Keeping
John Kerkkonen
Linda Kerkkonen
Alice Kimoff
Randy McCormick
C. D. Macdougall
Gary McDougall
Ian McEwan
  (pseudonym)

Shane McPherson
Randy Manuel
Terry Mattice
Ken Mohammed
Blair Morris
Pamela Oulton
  (pseudonym)
Victor Oulton
  (pseudonym)
Harvey Ratson
David Raun
John Reilly
Charlie Richmond
A.C. (Fred) Rogers
Maryann Rogodzinski
David Ross
Barry Schanehorn
Jessie Schrader
Sharon Seymour
Al Sholund
Leslie Simmons
  (pseudonym)
Maureen Simpson
  (pseudonym)
Marilyn Dunsmore
  Strilchuk
Peter Vanderlugt
Theresa Watkins
Mark Whyte
David Willford
Debbie Yurkoski

# Index